DRIVING HOME

MY UNFORGETTABLE SUPER BOWL RUN

JEROME BETTIS
with Teresa Varley

TRIUMPH
BOOKS
CHICAGO

Library of Congress Cataloging-in-Publication Data

Bettis, Jerome.
  Driving home : my unforgettable super bowl run / Jerome Bettis.
    p. cm.
  ISBN-13: 978-1-57243-838-5
  ISBN-10: 1-57243-838-X
  1. Bettis, Jerome. 2. Football players—United States. 3. Super Bowl (40th : 2006 : Detroit, Mich.) I. Title.
  GV939.B48A3 2006
  796.332092—dc22

                         2006010713

This book is available in quantity at special discounts for your group or organization. For further information, contact:

Triumph Books
542 South Dearborn Street
Suite 750
Chicago, Illinois 60605
(312) 939-3330
Fax (312) 663-3557

Printed in U.S.A.
ISBN-13: 978-1-57243-838-5
ISBN-10: 1-57243-838-X
Design by Wagner Donovan Design

Photos except where otherwise noted copyright © *Pittsburgh Post-Gazette*, 2006, all rights reserved. Reprinted with permission.

All photos by Peter Diana/*Pittsburgh Post-Gazette* unless otherwise indicated.

CONTENTS

Foreword

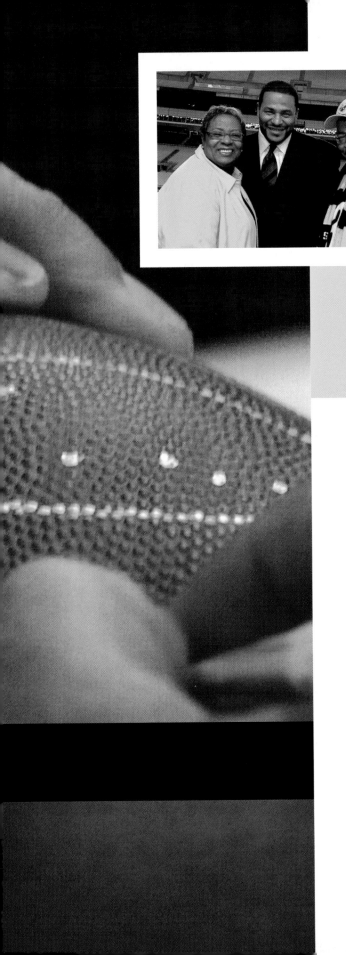

Foreword by Gladys and John Bettis

When the Steelers and Jerome began their Super Bowl run in 2006, friends told us to just relax and enjoy the ride. Well, it's not easy to relax when you know that your son is aiming for the most dramatic moment of his career—coming home to win the championship of professional football.

But our friends were right.

From Mackenzie High School in Detroit to Notre Dame to the Los Angeles Rams and Pittsburgh Steelers: what a wonderful ride it's been.

GLADYS: I didn't want him to play football, and I was terrified every time Jerome stepped on the field. That's why we went to almost every one of his games. At first, I was practically always sitting in the stands with an inhaler of his clutched in my hand. I knew the risks and how serious asthma can be.

JOHN: My wife is a lot more emotional than I am. I knew how much football meant to Jerome and how determined he was to play. I was never one to go against her decisions on raising our children, but Jerome and I double-teamed her on this one.

GLADYS: If he wanted to play sports I encouraged him to go into bowling. That was nice and safe, and he was good at it, too. I really thought Jerome would end up with an academic scholarship.

But my brother, Leroy Bougard, was watching him play in a pickup game one day. Jerome was only in the eighth grade or so, but my brother said he was a natural. He told us that Jerome already was bigger than boys four years older than he was, and quicker and faster, too. I didn't want to believe him. But Leroy was a high school coach in Detroit, and he knew how to spot talent.

JOHN: We counted them up, and I think we missed all of two games in his entire career, high school to pro. Even after Gladys knew he'd be all right and stopped worrying so much, we didn't want to get out of the habit of seeing him play.

We once had a car that could barely make it out of the city. So Gladys's sister, Gloria Bettis, let us use a van that belonged to the company she worked for. We just had to get it back in the lot by Sunday night. Let's just say we ran up a lot of miles in that borrowed van. And when it broke down on us on the drive home one weekend, that was a bad moment.

GLADYS: When Jerome ran onto the field in Detroit for the start of the Super Bowl, my emotions got the best of me. I was trembling all over. I was wiping away tears that whole game. But I knew his teammates wouldn't let him down. Besides, we had everyone in Pittsburgh, everyone in Detroit, and everyone from Notre Dame praying for him. That's a lot of prayers. How could the Steelers lose?

JOHN: I usually don't say much during a game and just watch the clock tick down to triple zero. But in that Indianapolis game, after Jerome fumbled at the goal line, I couldn't bear to watch. The Colts were moving in to tie it with a field goal, and their kicker never missed. When he did, that's when I knew we were going all the way. But I still had to see that last triple zero.

GLADYS: If I've learned one thing from this whole experience, it's to advise moms who have kids with asthma to let 'em play. Watch over your children, make sure they take their medication, but don't hold them back if they truly love the game. Don't let asthma stop them. The medications are much better now than they were when Jerome was younger, and I'll never regret the decision we made.

JOHN: When Jerome left for college, I took him aside and told him this: "Son, I don't have much to give you except a name, but it's a clean name. It's never been on any police blotter, and it's never caused any trouble. See that you take care of it."

GLADYS: I'd say he did, wouldn't you?

—*Gladys and John Bettis*

Acknowledgments

First and foremost, I would like to thank God for giving me such a blessed life.

A special thank you to my wife, Trameka, for putting up with all this.

I also would like to thank my mother and father for all the love they showered me with.

Thank you to the Steelers organization for allowing an all-access pass for the project. Teresa Varley, thank you for being patient with me throughout the process. Peter Diana, thanks for such great shots.

Thanks Jahmal Dokes for being my ace in the hole! And to everyone who helped make this book so special.

And last but not least, special thanks to the Steelers Nation for all the support that you have given me. I shall always bleed black and gold. Thank you!

—*the Bus, No. 36*

This Was Going to Be It

Let's start with one of my most disappointing moments in professional sports. The Steelers and I had high hopes and Super Bowl dreams in the 2004 season, and going into the AFC Championship in January 2005, everything was going our way. We were playing the New England Patriots at home, and the atmosphere was electric. We were confident because we had beaten them during the regular season, and we were filled with excitement and anticipation. For me personally, it looked like a trip to the Super Bowl might be the capstone to my career. We were primed and ready to go. We were in our stadium, Heinz Field, and everything was set up for us to go to the Super Bowl.

Unfortunately, we came out flat and the game got away from us early. It was one of those games where you just scratch your head and wonder what went wrong. We fought hard, but we were always down. Ultimately the clock became our enemy.

I was on the sideline thinking, "I can't believe this is happening. This was supposed to be a celebration. This was supposed to be one of those crowning achievements in my last year—going to the Super Bowl." I was looking at the seconds ticking away, asking myself what happened.

Ben Roethlisberger came over and, as a team leader, I was trying to console him. I told him it's only one game, we'll bounce back—all the things you say in a situation like that. But in the back of my mind I was thinking this would be the one and only time I'd ever be this close. Of course, I didn't want to tell Ben that. I wanted to be a strong shoulder for him. He looked at me, and I'll never forget what he said. He said, "Give me one more year, and I promise you I will get you to the Super Bowl." I kind of shrugged it off as a young guy being a young guy and wanting to say the right thing. But I did say, "I'm going to hold you to that."

After the game I went out onto the field and shook hands with the Patriots. I shook Bill Belichick's hand, and he told me I was one of the best running backs who ever played the game. That was a real compliment, and it meant a lot to me. Charlie Weis, the newly hired coach at Notre Dame, came over and told me he would need my help with Notre Dame the next season. That was bittersweet, but Notre Dame is my alma mater, so I told him I'd do whatever I could for him, even though he had just beaten us to go to the Super Bowl.

Leaving the field, I was disappointed, kind of disgusted, but still thinking that this had been an incredible ride. I didn't know for sure if that was going to be the last game, but I figured that it would be. I was trying to cherish the moment as much as I could, even though I was disappointed. I got into the locker room and was really frustrated, looking at everything as if seeing it for the last time. I will never forget the long walk to the postgame press conference where I had to talk about the loss. It was a terrible moment. I kept thinking about what might have been. I had attained so much in my career, and the Super Bowl was going to be the one thing to elude me.

I went home and just sulked. It took a while to get over it. It was a bad game, a real bad game. I was able to come to the realization, though, that I was okay with it. As crazy as it may seem, I was able to find some comfort in the fact that it had all come to an end.

The day after the game I addressed the team. I told them I appreciated how much they meant to me, how thankful I was to have that great bunch of guys as teammates. I got an opportunity later to see some footage of Hines Ward talking to the media, and he was crying, not knowing if I would be back and feeling bad that I might never get that Super Bowl ring. I think that was the turning point for me. That really struck a cord with me and made me start thinking.

I went to the Pro Bowl a few weeks later, and there were a bunch of guys in the game and at least another 10 guys who came just to be a part of it. They kept talking to me, hammering me that I needed to come back, to try one more time. I started to give it some serious thought. It was being with the guys at the Pro Bowl that really did a number on me, that really made me want to give it one more year, that helped me make the fateful decision to come back and see if Ben could indeed fulfill the promise he had made to me.

2005 TRAINING CAMP

I was really looking forward to getting to camp in 2005, but I approached it with mixed emotions because I was pretty sure it would be my last year. I was also in a totally different frame of mind because for the first time, I had a daughter to provide for. Unfortunately the rigorous camp schedule didn't allow time for me to see her, and that

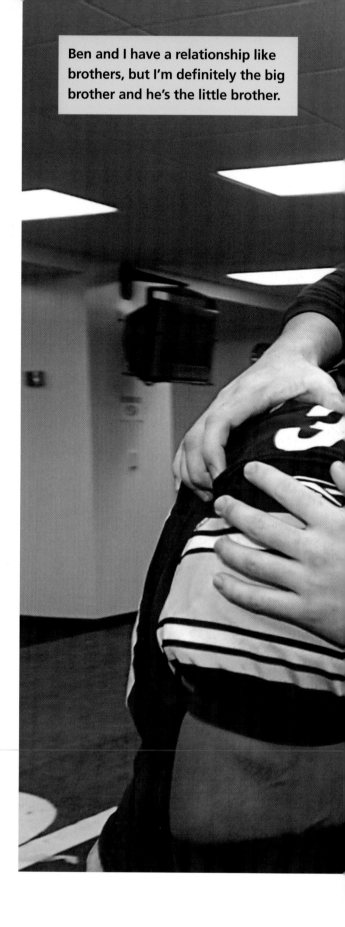

Ben and I have a relationship like brothers, but I'm definitely the big brother and he's the little brother.

BETTIS ON BEN ROETHLISBERGER

When Ben got here I took on the role of a big brother. Warren Moon told him to look me up when he got in town, that I would help him out and guide him. When he got here he asked me to come by and talk to him, so I did. We talked, and I gave him an understanding of what to expect as a first-rounder. I told him I was a former first-round pick, even though it was quite a few years ago, and I understood the expectations and everything that was being asked of him. I told him some of the things he needed to expect to do, things to be careful of as a young guy. The relationship developed from the standpoint of my being a big brother, telling him what to do, what not to do, to speak only when spoken to as a rookie, those kinds of things.

He is definitely the little brother. He is always after me trying to get the upper hand and get back at me. I am always getting on him, so whenever he has the opportunity to get on me, he does that.

Leaving the field with Ben Roethlisberger (center) and Dan Kreider (No. 35) after my five-yard touchdown run in the AFC Championship game against the Patriots on January 23, 2005. We came out flat and never recovered, which made for an awfully long and frustrating off-season.

Photo courtesy of AP/Wide World Photos.

was difficult for me. In previous years there might have been an injury or another type of distraction, but it was still all football all the time in camp. This year, it seemed for the first time football didn't mean as much. It was definitely a different feeling.

When I got to Latrobe, I was bombarded with questions about Hines Ward and his possible holdout, but I negotiated my way through the reporters as quickly as possible and made it to my dorm room ready to begin my 13th camp.

At our first practice it was obvious right away that Hines and his personality were not out there on the field. He and I like to play this game where we hit each other in the ribs when we're not paying attention. Without him, I didn't have anyone to get my mind off training camp practice. I had to focus in a different way, and it didn't seem as much fun. I went through the first day of practice and it was hot, but I was still excited to be there thinking I might be doing all this for the last time. There was a lot of excitement and fanfare that first day, as always.

One of the drills we go through in camp is the "backs on backers," where the running backs are trying to block the linebackers when they are blitzing the quarterback. It's an unfair drill because the defensive player has the whole field to get around you, whereas in an actual game he has only a small window because of the offensive line. It's unrealistic, but it shows your toughness as a running back and your willingness to put your head in there and take a hit from the linebacker. The linebackers would try to take advantage of the running backs by putting their moves on us, so we had to come up with a strategy to outsmart them by helping each other anticipate who was coming and from which direction. It didn't always work.

It's a drill of pride. It's one of those drills that if you lose, your whole practice is headed south. If you win, the practice tends to be more upbeat, because the running backs are the heart and soul of this football team, especially the offense. When we do well it seems like the day goes well. When we do badly, it seems like bad things tend to follow in the full practice.

It gets loud, too. When the running backs are on top, we are definitely the loudest. I probably get a little bit louder than I should sometimes. That's just my emotional nature and love for the game getting the best of me. The defensive guys definitely want to shut me up.

This training camp was both good and bad. It was good because I was healthy going into camp; I felt great, and I was in great shape. What was bad, though, was that soon after we got there Duce Staley had to have surgery, and the load fell squarely on my shoulders. I had not expected

I was really looking forward to training camp in 2005. I was healthy, felt great, and in great shape, but I also was pretty sure it was going to be my last camp.

REFLECTIONS IN THE REARVIEW MIRROR

It's pretty amazing to think that I was able to end my football career by playing in (and winning) the biggest game of my life in the city where I grew up. Here I am at home in Detroit, taking my tricycle out for a spin at age two and a half, and getting ready for bed at age three. *Photos courtesy of the Bettis family.*

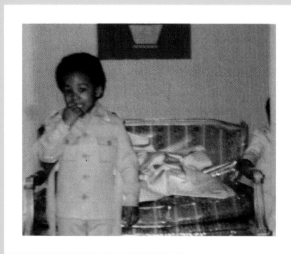

it, but I was prepared for it in the event that it did happen. I wasn't upset or anything; I was just surprised that it happened so early.

What was strange is that I was put in this protective shield because the coaches didn't want anything to happen to me during camp. It was understood that the guys weren't to bang on me during practice or try to tackle me to the ground. Also, in the first couple of preseason games, I played only about four or five plays, when usually as the starter you play a quarter or a half. There was a quick pull with me, and it was understandable. They wanted to be safe.

The fans are a big part of camp for us. When I go into the locker room to change after practice I kind of play with the crowd a little bit, just enjoying them and giving them an opportunity to interact with me as opposed to just signing some autographs. I give them the opportunity to decide which side I go to by seeing which side yells the loudest. It's fun for the fans, but it also makes me feel wanted. It feels good. Some of my teammates mess with me about it, calling me Hulk Hogan when I get them to yell, but everyone enjoys it.

During camp we get to meet a lot of kids and adults with special needs. It's always special when you can bring a little joy into someone's life, especially if it's someone who might be going through life-changing, or even life-threatening, circumstances. If you can use your celebrity to bring some joy, it's all worth it. When I get that opportunity I love it. I understand the responsibility that I have because of the recognition I've received on this team. It comes with the territory. I understand it and enjoy it. It gives me an opportunity to give back in a small way.

Our camp is held at St. Vincent College in Latrobe, Pennsylvania, and life in Latrobe is pretty quiet. There is not a whole lot to do, and that's probably better for us. It lets us focus. You don't have a lot of time in camp to do stuff anyway, but we did get a chance one evening to get away and enjoy things around Latrobe. Some of us went to ride go-carts and play putt-putt. It ended up getting pretty competitive, as you can imagine with a bunch of jocks. Doesn't matter what the sport is, as athletes, our competitive nature will always come to the fore whether on or off the football field. We played putt-putt, and unfortunately Ben Roethlisberger won, but I got even with him on the go-carts, where I was able to lap everyone. That was fun. It's a competitive spirit that we all have. It was great to get away from camp and do something fun, laugh and smile for a while, and for a small moment be away from football and enjoy your teammates.

Living in the dorm brings you back to reality. It's a small space that allows you to do only so much. It takes you back to your college days and the restrictions you had to live by. It's tough, especially now that

The fans are as big a part of training camp as anything. I would choose which side to go to to sign autographs by which side made the most noise. It was fun for the fans, but it also felt pretty good to hear all those people yelling for me.

DRIVING HOME

I have a family. But my dorm was pretty decked out, and I had some perks the other guys didn't have. For instance, I had a 42-inch plasma television, with DirecTV hooked up to it. I also had a full-size bed and refrigerator brought in there. I had a comfortable living space, to say the least. A lot of guys would come in and wonder how I was lucky enough to get this stuff. I told them it's not what you do, it's who you know.

During the downtime at camp, between practices and meetings, I watched a lot of television, and when I got bored with that I would wander around, going room to room picking on the other guys.

Some of the other guys liked to play the Madden video game challenge. They'd have tournaments, and I'd do the commentating for the games. We had a lot of fun with that. I don't play video games, though. I used to be a video game junkie, staying up all night playing video games and then trying to go to work. I realized that wasn't the healthiest thing for me to be doing. I went cold turkey and haven't touched the joystick since.

We also had a contest where we pitched quarters, between meetings or any time we got a five-minute break in the action. Usually, it would be me, Duce Staley, and Verron Haynes. Every night we would keep a record of who won that day. That was about the seventh or eighth year I was doing it, and I hadn't lost a year yet. I am the reigning champion of the quarter pitch.

I liked to ride my bike around camp, too. It was the same bike I had since my rookie year. I always had it at camp, so it became part of my ritual. It also gave me a chance to get myself going in the morning when we had an early practice. It let me get my body going with a low-impact workout. The problem is, every year it would turn up missing at camp, and 2005 was no exception. Turned out to be one of the assistant equipment managers who decided he wanted to mess with me some.

The food at camp has gotten a lot better. There was always ice cream, and I would usually sneak some back to my room in the evening for a late-night snack.

I went through the entire camp with the thought in mind that if this was to be my last year, I wanted to enjoy every part of it. I wanted to let it sink in, so the memories would be there for the rest of my life. It wasn't as agonizing as it usually was. I actually looked forward to the next day, and the next day, and the next. I wanted to take it all in.

When I left camp I didn't ask myself if I would be back. I was just happy to be heading home to sleep in my own bed. The one thing I did when I got on Route 30 heading home was look back in the rearview mirror and say to myself that that could be the last time I was looking at Latrobe. I just wanted to get a good picture of it in my mind.

THE PRESEASON

The preseason was tough for me, because I got hurt in the third game against the Redskins. When I got hurt I felt the pop. At first, I thought the referee might have thrown his flag and hit me in the back of the leg. Then a million thoughts started racing through my head: "If it's my Achilles, I'm out for the year. I never should have come back this year. No, maybe it's not the Achilles, thank goodness." When I got to the sideline, I realized it was my calf, but it was still going to be a while before I was back on the field.

I was a little bit discouraged because I was looking forward to starting the season off with a bang. Unfortunately, being sidelined like that made me feel like I let my teammates down. I wanted to be there and be someone they could count on until Staley got back. It was a frustrating feeling.

We played at Carolina the next week, and I didn't even make the trip. It was weird because for one of the first times I can remember I didn't go on the road to a game. It's something I did my whole career. It seemed very strange, and I didn't know what to do with myself. I went in for my normal treatments without thinking. But of course there weren't any trainers at the facility.

I decided I wanted to get out of the house to watch the game, so I went to a sports bar with a buddy who was in town. It was a different feeling, almost like an out-of-body experience, sitting there watching my team play on television. People in the restaurant didn't think it was me because of course they assumed I'd be at the game. Finally someone got up the nerve to ask me if I was Jerome Bettis. The whole experience made me wonder what it will be like to watch the Steelers when I am retired.

As I watched the game, I really paid attention to the running game, but I wasn't looking at just that. I was watching the whole game. Usually I just watch it from a running back's perspective, but this time I was looking at it as a fan. I was going through the emotional ups and downs of the game like any fan would, but obviously having a little more inside information about what was going on. It seemed a bit surreal. I could hear other people making critical comments when something went wrong on the field, and I wanted to let them know how wrong they were, but I decided it was better just to keep my mouth shut.

Missing the Action

Getting ready for the home opener against the Titans
was tough. I knew I wasn't going to be playing, so I tried to focus on
getting Willie Parker ready to play. I gave him some presnap reads and
a general idea of what to expect, and I threw in a few little tricks of the
trade I picked up over the years. I threw myself into that so I wouldn't
think about not playing.

Game day was pretty weird. My daughter was a little bit sick, which
caused me to be late to the stadium for the first time in my life, but it
was a situation where I decided my family had to come first. The day
turned out to be bittersweet for me because I had really looked forward
to it, but I wasn't playing. For the first time in my career, on opening
day I wasn't going to be in uniform. It was very eerie driving to the
stadium knowing I wasn't going to play.

I got to the stadium, and I didn't know what to do. I was lost without a
pregame ritual to go through, so when I got out onto the field before the
opening kickoff, I was a little depressed. I wanted to have my pads on. It
was the first time in a while that I was truly disappointed that I couldn't
be out there. In the preseason it was okay, and in practice it was okay.
But when that first game rolled around and everyone else put pads on, it
really hit me. It also made me appreciate how special it would be when I
could play again.

I had never watched an NFL game in person from anywhere but the
sideline, so I thought it might be kind of neat to sneak up to my suite
and actually watch opening day from a different vantage point. As I was
going to the suite, I got some quizzical looks from some fans, but I didn't
stop to explain.

Once again, it was a strange feeling to actually watch the players come
out and to hear the introductions from way up there. I felt so far
removed from playing football. It was another out-of-body experience,

BETTIS ON WILLIE PARKER

With Willie things were different. His first year I talked to him a little bit, but it went into warp speed when he became a starter. I told him what to expect, not only from an on-field standpoint, but also what he had to do off the field. It kind of became a 24-hour tutorial trying to help him with all of the tools he would need for the journey. I was in his ear quite a bit about things we needed to do. It was important. It was a long process, but a good one. I was able to give him a lot of the knowledge I have, rather than taking it with me. I think he got a lot better, and we as a team got a lot better as we started to figure things out.

I took pride in his accomplishments. As a player trying to give the information, I felt it was important for me to give it to him in a way that he understood it. When he went out and made use of it, it was really impressive, and that was the fun part. It made me understand I wasn't just wasting my breath talking to the guy, that he understood what I was saying and was using it. That made it fun.

Unable to help my teammates out on the field, I tried to focus on getting Willie Parker ready to play—and he was.

I'd hurt myself in the preseason game against Washington, so mentally preparing for the first few games of the regular season was tough. I felt pretty helpless, like I'd let my teammates down somehow.

GAME 1 VS. TENNESSEE, SEPTEMBER 11, 2005

	1	2	3	4	Score
Tennessee	7	0	0	0	7
Pittsburgh	7	13	14	0	34

watching everything happen as if it were in slow motion. It felt so weird. When it was time to start the game I got goose bumps. Watching football with myself not in the picture was extremely disappointing.

My family was all there, as always. They were really into the game and not paying any attention to me at all. It was like I wasn't there, and that was good. I wanted to just soak it all up by myself and get a feel for everything. It was good they were so involved in the game. It made me realize they are true football fans and not necessarily just fans of the Bus. It was good.

I didn't last long in the suite. After the opening kickoff, I watched the first couple of plays and was itching to get back down on the sideline with my teammates where I belonged. After the first drive I took off because I couldn't stand it anymore. I snuck back on the field, and once I got there, I felt good. I was excited and back to being a part of things. I'm still glad I went up to the suite, though, just for the one-time experience.

After the game started, my focus was on trying to figure out what the Titans were doing and what information I could give Willie that would be useful to him. I also watched the offense and defense, which I normally don't do. It was different being on the sideline that day. I had really, really been looking forward to playing.

The one fun thing was watching Willie. You see a guy who is really hungry, who wants to succeed. To see him go out there and do what he was able to do was a treat. We had spent time talking all week. Helping him get ready for the game and then seeing how he did was great.

The week before the game I didn't approach it the same way. I wasn't involved in practice because I was doing more rehab stuff. In meetings I wasn't as attentive as I normally was. On the test that we got on Saturday each week, I got a question wrong, which rarely happened. There were times I lost focus because I was not playing. For example, I may have fallen asleep once or twice when they were showing practice films in the meetings. I found it's hard to stay that focused all the time when you know you are not playing.

GAME 2 AT HOUSTON, SEPTEMBER 18, 2005

	1	2	3	4	Score
Pittsburgh	10	10	7	0	27
Houston	0	0	7	0	7

I've always been a presence in the locker room, whether it's joking around to keep people loose or getting guys emotionally fired up. During the time I was hurt I tried to be more of a teacher and find other ways to motivate the team.

It was also tough spending the extra time in the training room. You don't really want to be there. You have to get up earlier to get treatment before everyone comes in to do what they have to do. You're there earlier and you stay later. It's frustrating because you want to get better, but it's a slow process and you can't speed it up.

IT'S EASIER WHEN YOU WIN

The first game I was really, really happy that Willie was able to go in and give us the running game we needed to help us beat Tennessee. Next up was Houston on the road, and I was happy to see Willie do well in that game as well.

Then we came back the third week to play New England at Heinz Field. That was the game that was the biggest disappointment of all to me, because it was a game where I knew I could really help, I could really be very effective, and even though I was close to being ready to play, I couldn't be out there. That was the frustrating part. I felt good enough to play, but the coaches thought it was in my best interest to wait another week because we had a bye the following week. I felt totally helpless because I knew there were some instances where I could have made an impact, using the clock, pounding, and getting some of those tough yards when we needed them. That's what they pay me for, and I felt for the first time that I really let my teammates down. All I could think about was "what if" and "if only." Very frustrating.

It was tougher not being able to play in the Patriots game, because of the loss, than it was missing the first two wins. You think you can make a difference. A win is a win, with or without you, even if you think it might have been a bigger win with you. With a loss, you can't help but think you might have had an impact in the game that could have changed the outcome, even if it's only something I could have said in the huddle. So I tend to beat myself up after a tough loss when I'm not able to play.

When I was hurt I took on a different role. I took on the role of teacher and motivator. Since I couldn't lead by example I had to find other ways to lead. As I said, I tried to get with Willie to show him some of the tricks of the trade, and I got with some of the other guys and showed them what was necessary to take that next step to improve their game. I met with some of the offensive linemen and showed them some things that would help the running backs out and some things to look for. I tried to be a vocal leader and get the guys to follow by seeing my work ethic. Because I couldn't play, I had to find other ways to impact the team. I really tried to coach from experience.

I love to joke around in the locker room. I am a fire starter. I try to keep it going, keep it funny, keep things loose. I start trouble sometimes

It was definitely frustrating being hurt the first few games of the season, and it especially stung during the loss against New England, where I really could have helped the team by grinding out some yards and helping to control the clock.

GAME 3 VS. NEW ENGLAND, SEPTEMBER 25, 2005

	1	2	3	4	Score
New England	7	0	3	13	23
Pittsburgh	10	0	3	7	20

just to get guys emotionally charged and get their juices flowing. People know me by now, and they know I am always up to something and messing with guys. They have fun with it. Even when I wasn't playing I was like that. I kept the same type of approach in there.

Practice, though, was tough during those three weeks. When you miss practice and you know you aren't going to play, some of the things that the coaches say are kind of "blah, blah, blah." Everything is such a drawn-out process. Time moves at a glacial pace—like, tick-tock, tick-tock...hmmm, only four minutes gone by? Each step takes longer because you are not as focused mentally. When you are focused and involved, time goes fast. When you are not focused and you aren't paying attention, you are just there and everything takes a lot longer. It's a tough feeling.

DAD'S RETIREMENT DINNER

We had our bye week following the New England game, and I was able to attend a retirement dinner for my father in Detroit. He had worked for the city of Detroit for 32 years, and my mother put together the dinner and celebration to honor him. She waited for the bye week to do it so I could be there, and it turned out to be a wonderful little party with a lot of family, friends, and colleagues. Everyone was there. Some of the people I hadn't seen since I was a kid, and it was great to be around so many family members and friends. I got to hear stories about my dad that I hadn't heard before. The whole evening was designed to honor him, not roast him, and it was good to see everyone come in and pay homage to my father for all of the hard work he put in during his life.

I was happy I did come back for the 2005 season because I didn't want to retire before my father did. It was just a great event, and my father was happy and at peace with his decision to retire. So we all had a good time, and I came to a better understanding of his dilemma and the decision he had to make about his retirement. I had a newfound understanding for retirement and what it meant.

Looking at my father and his decision made me realize there comes a time when you just have to accept that it's over. There comes a time when you know you're ready, when you know you're done, when you know you've laced them up for the last time and you have to walk away from the game. When he walked away from his career he said, "This is it; I am done." For me to not have the certainty that I was really finished would have made a premature retirement a bad decision for me, and that's the uncertainty I had at the end of the playoffs after the 2004 season. If I had quit then, the desire to play would have continued to

My dad got a chance to experience life in my shoes while we shared a moment during a photo shoot for a magazine.

Fortunately, we had a bye week after the New England game, and I finally was able to get healthy. And Trameka and I got to show off Jada to friends and relatives.

Photo courtesy of the Bettis family.

REFLECTIONS IN THE REARVIEW MIRROR

Here I am at age seven, wearing what would be one of my first—but obviously not my last—uniforms, and at my eighth birthday party on February 16, 1980, entering into the glasses era. *Photos courtesy of the Bettis family.*

BETTIS ON HELPING AFTER HURRICANE KATRINA

Shortly after Hurricane Katrina, I got a call asking if I would appear on the *Today Show* to help Habitat for Humanity. They wanted me to help build some houses in New York that would be shipped to New Orleans for hurricane relief. I would be representing the Steelers. It was a great reason to do it. It took some convincing of my wife, Trameka, because she was going to have to travel to Detroit for my dad's retirement dinner by herself with the baby, but she agreed, so I was off to New York.

We had an early call time for the show, and I went with a friend of mine, a business partner who is about 10 or 12 years my senior. We got there and were working on the houses, just the two of us, when Al Roker from the *Today Show* turned and said, "Jerome Bettis and the Pittsburgh Steelers are here." I started laughing, thinking, if anybody asks, I'll just say my friend is our new kicker. Sorry, Jeff Reed, but you've been replaced just for today, just for the *Today Show*. Anyone who saw that show was probably thinking, "Who is this guy? What number is he? I don't see him on the roster or anywhere in the media guide."

We had fun, though. We got the hammer and nails and put some sections together. We actually had to take some apart, too. It's weird the way they build these houses and ship them off.

At the end of the show they brought up some of the Colorado Rockies and a couple of Olympic athletes, and then they pulled me right up there and said, "The Bus is here." Everyone recognized who I was, and they made a big deal about it. It was fun to be recognized like that in a major way and have people all over the country see that.

We also did an autograph session at Heinz Field, where autographs were sold to raise funds for the hurricane relief effort. It was important to be a part of that. It meant a lot to be able to help out, especially since we have teammates from the New Orleans area.

I'm always happy to pose with Trameka and our beautiful daughter, Jada. *Photo courtesy of the Bettis family.*

burn within me, and that's how I know my decision to come back for one more year was the right decision.

My father didn't talk to me about his decision. He just told me he was ready. When someone tells you they are ready, nine times out of 10 there is no turning back. I knew it was a decision that he alone could make. He has to wake up every day and live with the decision. It wasn't my place to question the decision as much as to understand it and live with it. I did understand that part. When my decision had to be made, only I could make it.

I was so proud of my dad at the dinner. When people come and pay homage like that it means you are a good person and that people respect you and what you did enough to come and share that with you. That's the way I looked at it. He is such a good person that people wanted to say thanks and show how much they appreciated it. As a son there is no better feeling than knowing that your dad is a great man and that he stood for something and meant a lot to a lot of people, because I know he means a lot to me.

It also was a chance to show my daughter, Jada, to all of our family. It was her first chance to meet a lot of the extended family, and it was a bit of a challenge. There were a lot of new faces, and it was tough early, but as the night wore on she took it in stride. I was a proud dad. A lot of people hadn't gotten the chance to see her and hold her. I was proud because this little girl is a product of me and my wife, Trameka, and I think she has all of the best parts of me. It made me proud to show her off.

Getting Back into the Swing of It

Our bye week after the Patriots loss allowed me the chance to get back and to get healthy. Finally, I was getting ready to come back and practice and play. I was so looking forward to being back on the field. I had that bad taste in my mouth from not being able to play in the New England game. We had a Monday night game against the Chargers. It was prime time, on the road in San Diego. I felt there was no better time to be coming back than to a premiere game.

I had an opportunity to get in the game early against the Chargers. The coaches wanted to get me in there early. The second play they called a screen pass. I said to myself, "I am a physical kind of runner; I am not really the screen type of guy." I'm thinking to myself that if I'm open on the screen, I'll have to do a lot of running, and I'm not exactly crazy about the idea. The first game back is always the toughest on you physically. You have practiced, but you haven't gone at game speed. Also, the conditioning is not there.

The first couple of plays it was okay, but then they gave me a pitch to the right, and I broke the pitch and went about 10 or 15 yards before I was tackled. I got up, and my lungs were burning. The game was electric, and I was trying hard to do my best. I went to the sideline then. From that point on I was in and out of the game. It was a close game, a tough game.

We got the ball back with a little over four minutes to play. We were down by one point. They put me in for the last series. For one, it felt good that the team and coaches had faith in me to have me in the game at the most pivotal moment. The game would be decided on that drive, and I was the running back. I ran the ball on first, then we threw on second and got to our own 47-yard line where it was a critical third-and-one situation. It was an opportunity for me to show what I am made of, show my worth. This is the reason I am here. Then—boom!—I plunge ahead for two yards and we get the first down. We run the ball a few more times and pass it, then we have another third-and-one situation from the Chargers' 42-yard line, and I am able to get that. The last game

I finally got to help the team during a critical situation late in a close game.

It was great to get back out onto the field against the Chargers in the Monday night game in San Diego.

against New England I wasn't able to provide those tough yards for the team and we lost. Here we were in a similar situation and I was able to go out and get those tough yards and we won. It was just a great feeling. To do it on such a stage as *Monday Night Football* was tremendous.

I left that game feeling pretty good about myself. It feels good to know that your role is important, that you are an important piece of the puzzle. So many times a guy comes back from an injury and he is not really an integral part of the team. It felt really good to hear the guys saying, "Hey, what took you so long, get your butt back in there." It was one of those things where they need you to go out and do what you do. It was a good feeling to know the team needed me to go out and do my job.

One of the amazing things about this game was the fans. Whenever we go across the country or a long way from Pittsburgh, the fan support is unbelievable. Everyone on the West Coast who is a Steelers fan understands this is their one opportunity to see their team. Fans came from everywhere: California, Seattle, Colorado, Arizona, Missouri, you name it. It was just incredible. You realize how revered the Steelers franchise is and how much they appreciate you. I saw so many "Bus" and "The Bus Is Back" signs. It made me proud to wear the black and gold. You understand how much it means to so many people. It's humbling in some ways. Everybody looks at us as a beacon of hope. It makes you proud that when you go out there you have twenty thousand fans on the road, which should never be the case in such a big game, but they are there and cheering for you and wearing your colors. It's just an amazing feeling.

When I did my dance after the run, I never really heard the crowd. I was in the zone, and I don't hear anything then. But I knew that they were reacting; I knew they were loving it, and it fired them up.

It would kill me if that many opposing fans were at games at Heinz Field. That would destroy me. The one image I have of Steelers fans is when we played the Jets in the playoff game in 2004 and it looked like every person in the stadium had a Terrible Towel. It was the prettiest thing I had ever seen while wearing a Steelers uniform. They were swinging them at the beginning of the game. That was the most awesome

GAME 4 AT SAN DIEGO, OCTOBER 10, 2005

	1	2	3	4	Score
Pittsburgh	0	14	0	10	24
San Diego	0	7	6	9	22

site I ever saw in that stadium. I was just taken aback by it. If it were ever the case that fans for the opposing team came to our stadium like that, it would be horrible. When we go into places like New York to play the Giants or to San Diego to play the Chargers and home teams are booed in their own stadium, it makes an impact on the game.

THE FIGHTING IRISH ARE BACK

At the end of the 2004 college season, Notre Dame fired their coach, Ty Willingham. I was very upset at the firing. It wasn't the fact that they fired him; it was how poorly it was handled. For the first time ever I was embarrassed to be a former player at Notre Dame.

The two leading contenders for the job seemed to be either Charlie Weis or our former quarterbacks coach with the Steelers, Tom Clements. Obviously my relationship was with Clements, so I was pushing for him.

I talked to the media about Coach Clements and the firing. It was a good opportunity for the media to ask questions. Being one of the higher-profile players who went to Notre Dame and being accessible to the media, everyone wanted my take on the situation. I didn't shy away from answering questions in the way I thought they should be answered.

Coach Weis got the job. He was the offensive coordinator with the New England Patriots at the time, and his getting the job pretty much coincided with us playing them in the 2004 AFC Championship game. After the game he and I met at the 50-yard line, and that's when he told me he was going to need me to help out at Notre Dame. I told him whatever he needed I would be happy to do.

Several months went by in the off-season, but the sting of losing the AFC Championship was still there. I got a phone call from someone in the Notre Dame football office, and they wanted me to coach the spring game. Because of other commitments, I couldn't do it, so Coach Weis asked me to call him. I was in Philadelphia working on an asthma campaign. My cell phone rang and it was Coach Weis. He asked me if I would be willing to talk to the team in the fall. As I said, I had told him I would do anything for him, so obviously that was a no-brainer.

Notre Dame was scheduled to play Pitt in Pittsburgh, at Heinz Field, so that's when I agreed to talk to the team. The team was staying at the Westin William Penn in downtown Pittsburgh. I went over there the night before the game to meet with Coach Weis first. It was the first time I had really been able to talk with him or spend any time with him.

Once he was hired I felt he was the right guy for the job in terms of experience and knowing offenses and how to beat defenses. I knew he would be pretty good. I didn't particularly care for him at first because

Notre Dame's new coach, Charlie Weis, invited me to talk to his team before a game against Pitt at Heinz Field. I went up to his hotel suite the night before and had a great time getting to know him and his family.

he beat up on us when he was with the Patriots and stopped us from going to the Super Bowl twice, and I was harboring some ill will. But after meeting him, my opinion of him changed completely. I realized he was a good guy, a guy who should be respected for his knowledge of the game and his ability to coach.

We went up to his suite, and his wife and son were up there with him. We sat down and had a good conversation. We went back and forth about the NFL and other topics. I had newfound respect for him after we sat and talked for a while. He has a great, lovely wife, and his son is a pretty neat kid.

Then we started talking about Notre Dame. He was telling me how he put the onus on the players and that they were part of the reason their former coach was fired. He told them that if they didn't want to accept responsibility for that, then they weren't being realistic with themselves.

It was shocking to hear him say that. Usually a coach's approach is to emphasize the start of a new era, and they tiptoe around the controversial stuff that might have happened in the past. Instead, Coach Weis threw it out there so they could understand what was happening. He told them that if they wanted him fired, all they had to do was lose six games a year for the next three years and he'd be gone, too. He shocked them with a big dose of realism, and that was impressive.

We sat there in his suite and really got to know each other. We talked about his experience coaching and my experience at Notre Dame. We developed a mutual respect and the beginning of a good relationship.

He then asked me to come down and talk to the team. I am usually comfortable speaking in front of groups, but this time I was a little apprehensive. I wasn't exactly uncomfortable, but I was still a little nervous. I got up in front of the players and talked to them. My message was really simple. I told them to remember this was the same game they played when they were 10 years old and dominated then, and it's no different now. It's the same game they had been playing all their lives. I told them not to overcomplicate things, to just go out there and play. That's the approach I have taken my whole career. I didn't become too cerebral with the game in terms of trying to know so much that I lose sight of just making plays and being spontaneous out there on the field.

Talking to the guys, I felt comfortable. I felt relieved about the way I was able to communicate with them and explain things to them. I told them about the frustrating loss in the AFC Championship game, and I had the chance to really talk to them as men, not looking down at them but as peers. That was really good. Unfortunately, I didn't get a chance

I was actually a little nervous before talking to the team, but my message was simple: it's the same game we've been playing all our lives; just go out there and play the way you've always played it.

to talk to any of the guys one-on-one because they had more meetings after that.

The next day was game day, and it was a game I was really looking forward to. Pitt was ranked in the top 25 in the country. With Notre Dame at that point in the season you still didn't know what you were going to see out of them. I decided to go down on the field for the game. I was down there and it was a strange sensation, as it took me back to where my college football career began. I was looking at those helmets and jerseys and kind of reminiscing. I reflected on where I am in my career now and where I was when I played against Pitt when I was in college. It took me back to 1990 when I was a freshman and we played Pitt. It was pretty unique. I was just a freshman then, and I didn't know what was going on. Now I was watching them play Pitt and I was at the tail end of my career professionally. It was a unique experience.

Notre Dame won the game 42–21. For them to beat Pitt the way they did by running the ball, with 275 yards rushing, it brought back memories of the Notre Dame of years past. I just felt so proud that I wore that helmet and had *ND* on my sleeve when I was coming up. For one day Notre Dame was king of the hill, and it was a great day.

It was a unique feeling being at that game. Most of the people there were Pitt fans, but they were also Steelers fans, so they had a warm response for me. Even though I was with the opposing team, it was one of those things where they couldn't boo me because I play for the Steelers. The fans were in a bind trying to figure out how to acknowledge me. Do they acknowledge me as Jerome Bettis who plays for the Steelers, or Jerome Bettis the former Notre Dame player? I got nothing but positive responses.

It was so fun to watch Notre Dame play throughout the 2005 season, especially watching them beat Michigan. I came into the Steelers meetings that Saturday night at the hotel, and I was the proudest guy in the room. I had my Notre Dame hat on, I had my Notre Dame shirt on, and I was looking for our Michigan guys. Coach Cowher got up to start the team meeting, but before he could say anything, I got up and sang the Notre Dame fight song. Coach tried to stop me, but I told him I couldn't stop in the middle of the fight song. At that moment I was the proudest guy in the world, but I think I developed a lot of enemies that day.

Game after game, win after win, everything was going great for Notre Dame. Everyone deferred to me, asking questions about my Irish. It was a great feeling.

And then USC came to town. I was at home, lying in bed sleeping, when I woke up in a panic, thinking I had missed the start of the game.

Whatever I said must have worked because the Irish trounced Pitt 42–21 and went on to have a fabulous season for Coach Weis. I know I'm not the only one who's really excited about the future at Notre Dame.

I went downstairs to watch the game with my parents. For most of the game it was a seesaw battle: Notre Dame would score, then USC would score. It looked as though it was going to go down to the wire. In the last few minutes, Notre Dame scored to go ahead, and all they had to do was hold USC to win, but on fourth down Matt Leinart of USC threw a 40-yard completion for a key first down. Then, at the most crucial and exciting moment of the game, I had to leave to go to the hotel for our team meeting. I couldn't be late. As soon as I got in the car I called my father to ask what was happening. He told me USC had fumbled the ball out of bounds, as time ran out. He started yelling, "It's over, it's over. He fumbled out of bounds, and there is no time on the clock." I was going crazy and nearly crashed my car. Then he said, "Wait a minute; they put more time on the clock." And then I remember him telling me, "It's over, they lost." Those words rang in my head. He didn't explain what happened. He just said, "It's over, they lost." It was devastating, heartbreaking. It's over, they lost. There was a quarterback sneak and Reggie Bush pushed Leinart into the end zone. It's over, they lost. The words kept pounding in my head. It was like a day of mourning. An incredible sense of sadness swept through me. It was devastating. Just in case, I had brought my Notre Dame hat and shirt with me to wear again and was ready to reprise the fight song in front of the team. I was hoping for one more shining moment, but it wasn't meant to be.

I got to the team meeting and 52 guys were looking at me trying to contain their smirks, and Coach Cowher was grinning from ear to ear. We got into the meeting room and before Coach could start the meeting, the defensive players got Troy Polamalu, who went to USC, to get up and sing the USC fight song, much to my chagrin. It was the lowest I had felt in a long time. I had to suck it up, hold my head up, and go forward. It was a very disappointing day for me.

On top of that, I had made a bet with Troy that the loser had to wear the other team's gear. It was bad for two reasons. One, I had to wear USC colors all day, for an entire day. Two, I had to go to the mall and buy a USC shirt to fit me. Nothing Troy had would fit me. I had to lower myself and go into a mall and spend my own money to buy a USC shirt, which I then had to wear the entire day. It was the lowest time of the Notre Dame season by far. But being a man of my word I went to the mall where everybody there was wondering why I was buying USC stuff. I went in and bought the shirt and left without saying a word. I had disgust written all over my face. I came in the next morning and wore the shirt all day. After the day was over I took the shirt and balled it up and threw it in Troy's locker never to be seen again.

It seemed like everybody took pleasure in seeing me in a USC shirt, even people who had no affiliation with USC. It felt like everyone was against me and Notre Dame. It was very frustrating. It truly seemed like everyone in the building enjoyed seeing me in a USC shirt.

At least when Notre Dame beat Michigan the Michigan guys had to wear Notre Dame gear. They were disappointed, but they knew deep down they couldn't beat Notre Dame.

It's great to expect to win every week, and that's the really fun part that Notre Dame had been missing for so long. Every week to be able to bet on your team and say, "We are going to win," and to have that faith, that was fun. It had been a lot of years since we were able to say we were going to beat USC and not be just blowing smoke, saying that knowing we were playing the number one team in the country. That's something Notre Dame hadn't been able to do in a long time.

College football in general gains in many ways when Notre Dame is winning. Notre Dame attracts a lot of attention whether it's good or bad. When they are on the map it makes for good football on Saturdays. It also creates a national drama about what is going to happen with bowl situations, rankings, rivalries, and big games. Notre Dame has a history of not shying away from the best teams in the country. Every year they play the best teams regardless of what kind of team they have. It says a lot about what kind of team they are and what they believe in. When they are winning, they factor in heavily into the national championship, and I pay more attention to what is going on, too. Life is busier at home now with my daughter and wife, and my time is more limited than it used to be, but I still make time to find out about Notre Dame and follow things during the week and on game day.

I am really excited about the future of Notre Dame football. They signed Coach Weis to a 10-year extension. Initially I thought it was a little premature, but with the NFL lurking in the background I think it was probably a smart thing to do, to lock him up and make sure he doesn't go anywhere for a long time.

It's fun again to say I went to Notre Dame and to be proud of it. It's been a proud time for everyone who went to Notre Dame.

REFLECTIONS IN THE REARVIEW MIRROR

That's me on the left at age eight, with my cousin Brandon (age seven) and my brother John (age 12), striking our toughest poses for the camera. And me again at age nine—but not looking quite so tough in this one. *Photos courtesy of the Bettis family.*

4 My Biggest Disappointment

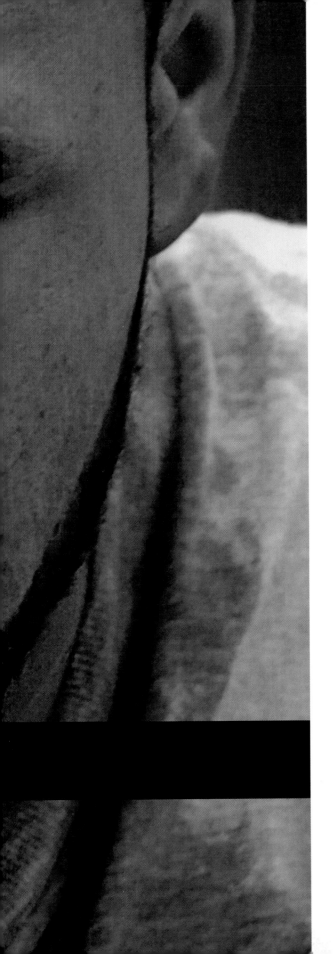

The week after the Chargers game we played Jacksonville. I thought this game would be business as usual for me. I didn't think anything would be different. I thought my role would be the same as it was the week before. I thought I would get a little bit more work because everything went well the week prior.

I got the opportunity to get in the game early, but I didn't have much success. I left the game without having gotten much work done during the first half. The second half came, and it went pretty much like the first half—not much excitement, not too many opportunities. It was a tough game, a real back-and-forth game. We were fighting back the majority of the game. We got a break near the end of the game when we stopped them from finishing a game-winning drive, and we went into overtime.

Overtime is a weird situation. The team that wins the coin flip determines possession, and the winner of the flip the majority of the time wins the football game. It was a big coin toss. We won it and elected to get the ball.

It was a big moment for us. They kicked off to us, and Quincy Morgan broke off a great kickoff return back to their 26-yard line. At that moment I forgot all about the subpar game I'd had up to that point because this was my opportunity. We needed only two, three, or maybe four yards at the most to set us up for a field-goal try. This was my role, the time they always turned to me. Instead, they brought in Willie. On the first play they ran him wide left. He got hit and fumbled, but recovered it himself, losing three yards on the play. I was thinking, "Okay Willie, that's all right." Then it was second down, and I was sure they'd want me in.

Just the week before Coach Cowher said that there were two things he could always count on: one, that I don't go backward, and two, that I don't fumble the football. I thought this would be the opportunity for them to right the wrong of not putting me in there on first down to pound the ball in there.

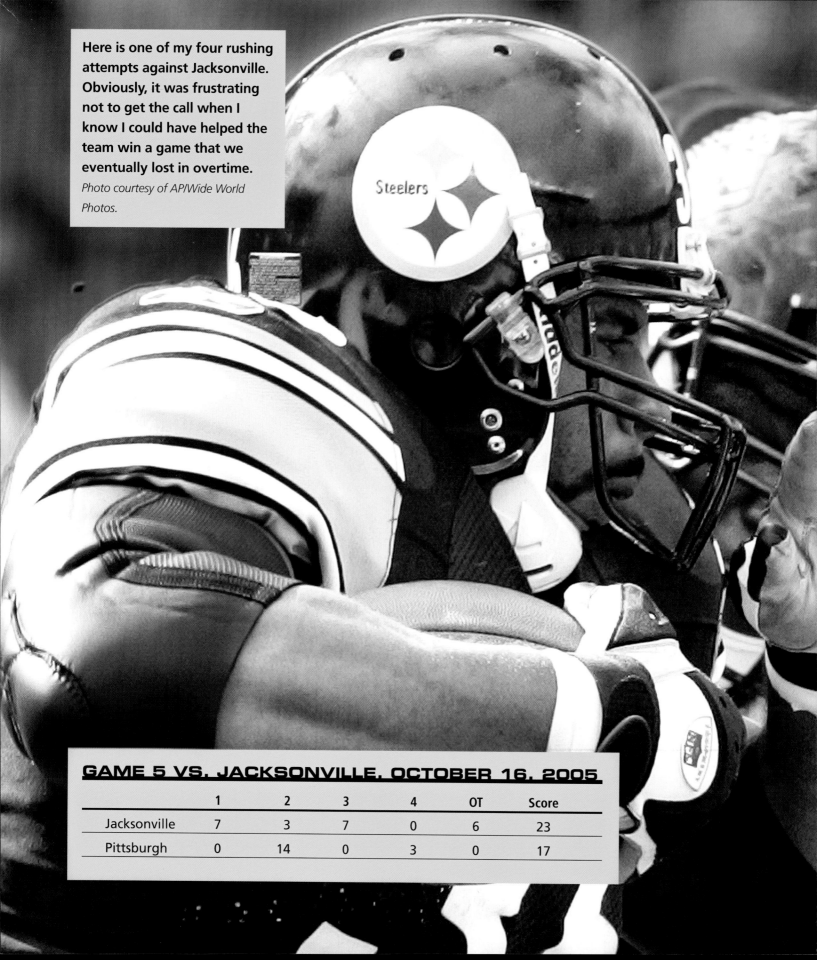

Here is one of my four rushing attempts against Jacksonville. Obviously, it was frustrating not to get the call when I know I could have helped the team win a game that we eventually lost in overtime.

Photo courtesy of AP/Wide World Photos.

GAME 5 VS. JACKSONVILLE, OCTOBER 16, 2005

	1	2	3	4	OT	Score
Jacksonville	7	3	7	0	6	23
Pittsburgh	0	14	0	3	0	17

On second down they ran the ball to Willie again, and he got two yards back. On third down they tried to run the football again, and Tommy Maddox fumbled the football and Jacksonville recovered. I'm not going to lie to you. At that moment I felt angry and betrayed. There's no way we should have been running that fancy play on third down when Maddox coughed up the football.

We went on to lose the game later when Tommy threw an interception and they returned it for a touchdown.

Before they had sent Willie in on first down, after the kickoff return, a lot of the guys on the team, assuming I'd be in there, were saying, "Let's go, Bus. Seal the deal." Joey Porter came over to me and said, "Let's go." I told him I wasn't in there. He shook his head and couldn't believe it. Duce Staley came over and told me to just go into the game. I told him I couldn't do that, that's not how we work. A lot of people were frustrated that I wasn't in the game.

When I saw Maddox had fumbled on third down, I was livid. In the same situation a week earlier they had given me the ball and I came through, and now they didn't even give me the opportunity. That's my role. I'm saying to myself if I don't get the ball in this situation, what am I on the team for?

When you get close and you need a field goal, you go to your field-goal kicker. When you have to punt the football, you go to your punter. When you have to throw the ball, you tell the quarterback to throw it. When you need to run the ball, you give it to the running back. When you need short yardage, you give it to me. That's my role.

I felt betrayed because that was the role they had assigned to me, the thing I had been relegated to. I don't have a problem with that, but then give me the ball in this situation. It was one of the most frustrating things I ever experienced on or off the football field. I could have made a difference, but I wasn't allowed to, and that was the part that hurt the most. Never had there been a situation that was so perfect for me, and they didn't use me. That had never, ever happened before. That was the toughest part.

It took everything I had not to blow a gasket in the postgame interviews. I hurried up, took a shower, and made sure I was one of the first ones to leave. I didn't want to say anything that I would regret the next day. The media came to me with questions, but I knew I couldn't say what I felt. I just bottled it up and didn't say much. I got the heck out of there.

When I left the stadium I just kept it all in and dealt with it my own way. It may not have been the best thing to do, but it's what I needed to do. I tried to analyze it internally. As much as I tried, I couldn't make sense of it.

I knew I was justified in my thoughts immediately, but hearing all of the comments after the game, the next day and so forth, made me realize that pretty much everyone else agreed with me. Last time they used me like that, the outcome was positive. This time they didn't use me, and the outcome was negative. I didn't feel vindicated because we lost the game. It wasn't me against the coaches. Everyone could see it, though. They knew what should have happened. It was more frustrating when people who weren't involved in the decision making could see it. That made it that much harder to deal with.

The Wednesday after the game, I went in and sat down to talk to Coach Cowher. The first thing Coach said was that I should have been in the game. He said it was his fault ultimately as the head coach of the football team because it's his responsibility to manage everything. He said in that situation he felt other coaches should have suggested or just told me to go out there, but he took responsibility for the decision because, as he said, it's his team. He didn't make the call, and he wanted to apologize to me for it.

I had only two things to say to him. First, I agreed the assistant coaches should have come to him and told him to put me in: the offensive coordinator first, my running backs coach second, and the assistant head coach, the line coach, third. All three of them should have demanded that I be on the field. Second, I told him he had an opportunity to make it right after the first down and still didn't, which compounded the situation. I felt as though it had been done purposely and intentionally. It wasn't a mistake or an oversight but what they wanted to do. It failed, and we paid the price. I wanted him to know what I felt had happened and shouldn't have happened. He understood that and apologized again.

It helped to know that he knew it was wrong. It was my role. Let me do my job. It felt good that he understood that I should have been in there, and they dropped the ball, so to speak. But it didn't change the fact that we lost the game, and that still hurt.

Coach Dick Hoak apologized to me after that, too. He said he felt like he let me down, that I should have been in the game. He was apologetic, and I appreciated that.

DOWN, BUT NOT OUT

It was time to get back in the win column, and we had a big game against the Bengals to get ready for. They were 5–1 going into the game and leading us in the AFC North. For the first time the Bengals didn't say much before the game. They were the favorites going into the game, and I don't think that has ever happened as long as I have been playing. There was a lot of hoopla around the game. It was a big game—the

Hines Ward and Coach Cowher look on in disbelief after Tommy Maddox's fumble in overtime against the Jaguars. *Photo courtesy of AP/Wide World Photos.*

BETTIS ON BILL COWHER

It's been a really good relationship between me and Bill. We've had our ups and downs, but it was never bad and always an open relationship. If I had a problem or an issue to talk about, his door was always open. He would talk to me as well, and we often talked about more than football. He would talk to me about issues with the team and at times use me as a liaison between him and the players. He would ask me what the thinking was in the locker room, what guys wanted to do, and he would really confide in me on a lot of issues that a player normally wouldn't know about. Our relationship has been great the whole time I have been in Pittsburgh.

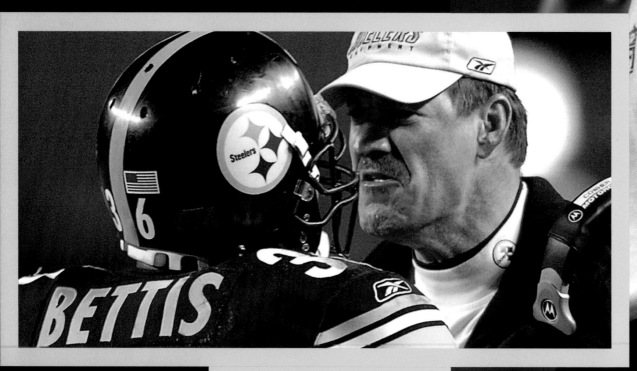

Any coach and player who've been together as long as Bill and I have are going to have their ups and downs, but our relationship has been great the whole time I've been in Pittsburgh.

GAME 6 AT CINCINNATI, OCTOBER 23, 2005

	1	2	3	4	Score
Pittsburgh	0	7	17	3	27
Cincinnati	3	3	0	7	13

biggest game in Cincinnati in 15 years. It was one of those things where you say, okay, let's see what Cincinnati has got. Having been here 10 years and having dominated them as thoroughly as we had—and I personally had more success against that franchise than against any other team—I felt confident that we would win the football game. I think that was part of the problem. It was hard for Cincinnati to beat us because, for the most part, when we play them we believe we are going to beat them and they believe they are going to lose.

For us it was business as usual. It was the Bengals this week. We didn't think of it as a big game. All the hype about it being a big game was coming from their side. We knew the importance; we knew if we lost to them we would be two and a half games back in our division. That's as far as we thought. We were looking at the division race and knew we couldn't let them be that far up in the division. That was our central concern. It wasn't us beating the Bengals. It was us not letting them get up like that in the division. They were looking at it as a statement game, their coming-out party, to announce that they had arrived. Everyone felt it was Cincinnati's time to show that they were the team to beat. We were a barometer for them.

Everyone came out all hyped up for the game. The Bengals had two big drives to start the game, but they got only three points out of them. They did have the two good drives down into our territory, though. We responded by scoring a touchdown and making some things happen early on in the game. Everything was going according to plan. I was having success. I think it was a concerted effort on the coaches' part to get me in the game early, and it paid off. On the initial drive for which I was in the game, we went in and scored the touchdown.

There was a key play on the goal line, a play-action fake to me. The Bengals were focused on me. Heath Miller was in the back of the end zone wide open. The whole defense expected me to get the football. The defense knows my role as much as the offense does. Everything kept going according to plan, and we kept on rolling, getting a touchdown for our efforts.

In the second half there was a pivotal third down. The score was 17–6 at that point, with us leading. It was third-and-three at the Bengals' 25-yard line. I remember vividly in the huddle looking at the sticks and seeing third-and-three. I was thinking that we had the wrong personnel on the field. Usually in a third-down situation, unless it's third-and-one, I am not in the game. This was a long third-and-three. They called a play in, and I figured I would have to block, but they called a run. I was thinking, "Third-and-three—that's a lot of yardage to pick up on third down." I knew I had to find a way to get the first down. They gave me the ball, and initially—boom!—one guy stopped me and I kind of bent over another guy, but I knew I wasn't down. I was in an awkward position, but I wasn't down. I tried to spin off and forge again. I was

Joey Porter celebrates a sack with Da Boot.

Photo courtesy of AP/Wide World Photos.

BETTIS ON JOEY PORTER

Joey and I have a unique relationship. He got with me a few years ago and asked me how I did it. He wanted the blueprint for success the way I understood it. I would tell him little things that were important for him to do. I told him to name his little kick, so he called it Da Boot. I told him to get it trademarked and get a logo like I did with the Bus. He was thirsty for knowledge, and I felt it was important for me to pass on the information. He was always listening. He wanted to use everything to his advantage. He was willing to do whatever it took to create a good situation for himself. It let me know that I was doing something right, having someone like that come to me for help and advice.

digging and plowing, making sure I didn't get my knees on the ground. I was pushing the pile, turning, doing everything I could do to get an extra yard. Before you knew it, one yard had turned into two yards, two had turned into three, and by the time the whistle blew, I had gained four yards and a first down.

It was one of the best runs I ever had simply because of the importance of the first down in that instance. The fact that it was a third-and-three

I had a couple of big plays in the first game against the Bengals, who were 5–1 coming in and ready to prove to the world that they were for real.

situation, when I normally wouldn't be on the field, made me really proud that the coaches had enough confidence in me to call my number, and the fact that I came through also made me feel pretty good. That one play summed up my career in the sense that I had been down a lot, but never stayed down. I always fought, scrapped, and clawed my way for another yard or opportunity or chance.

Everybody was going crazy on the sideline. It was one of those moments when everyone seemed to sense the significance of the play. Everyone was going bananas. It was a good feeling to know a four-yard run would get that kind of applause from your teammates.

The Bengals are a team I always have had a lot of success against. This game was no exception. But right at the point when it was time for me to really take the game over, their rookie linebacker, Odell Thurman, got me. One of the offensive linemen went the wrong way, and Thurman came shooting in the gap. I dove to try to get away from him, and he hit my leg. When he hit my leg he hit my quadriceps muscle and split it, and I was done for the day. The frustrating thing was that it was at the time when we needed to impose our will to run the football. We were still able to do it, but that had been my signature, especially against this team. It bothered me a lot to get hurt in this game because Cincinnati is a team I was able to dominate my whole career.

After the hit, I was on the sideline trying to warm up. I wasn't sure how bad the injury was, but I wanted to get back out there because I knew I was leaving a lot of yards out on the field. I was thinking to myself that I had to be the unluckiest person in the world to get hurt just when I had the chance to rack up some pretty good stats. I got hurt in the preseason, and then the next opportunity I had to pound my name in the dirt, I got hurt again. It was frustrating because I knew it was the end of my day, and all I could do was watch the other running backs run through the defense.

It was a fairly quiet game. There wasn't a lot of talking on the field. It was a surprisingly quiet Cincinnati team. After the first two touchdowns I guess they knew they weren't going to win the football game. They were disappointed they didn't play as well as they thought they could in a big game. We, on the other hand, had been in that kind of game quite often. For them it was the first time in 15 years. There was an advantage with us in terms of big-game nerves.

After the Cincinnati game I came back in on Monday and my leg was not responding very well. On Tuesday I got treatment for it. On Wednesday I tried to run and jog and my leg did not respond. About 7:00 that night we went to St. Margaret's Hospital and found out there was a vertical tear. Initially we didn't know it was that significant. We

REFLECTIONS IN THE REARVIEW MIRROR

Looking pretty sharp in this family photo, with (back row, from left) cousins LeWanda and little Kim, sister Kim, cousin Jason, brother John, and myself, and (front row) cousins Jaron and Lasundres. I'm 12 years old in the photo below, which was taken on Easter. *Photos courtesy of the Bettis family.*

thought it was just a quad bruise, a helmet to the quad, which isn't that unusual, but now we knew it was a lot more serious than that. I didn't practice on Thursday or Friday.

Saturday we had our production meetings with the *Monday Night Football* crew. I was talking with John Madden, who asked me about my interviewing with NBC Sports for a possible job. I thought it was very hush-hush, that no one else really knew about it, but what I found out was that Madden knows a little bit about everything. He gave me a little advice and told me to be myself. He knew I was going for an interview the following Tuesday and gave me some good advice. He is a good broadcaster and gave me some great tips.

We had our normal team meetings and then had a night practice to prepare for the Monday game against the Ravens. I tried to practice, but it was pretty bad. I was limping around, struggling to get through practice, and I thought if I took some Tylenol or something I could make it through the game. Boy, was I wrong. My first play in the game I went down right on my quad. Bang. My leg felt like spaghetti. I picked myself up off the ground, and I knew I was hurt. I made my way over to the sideline and immediately tried to convince myself that it wasn't as bad as I thought, but I knew I was lying to myself. Luckily for me the coaches didn't send me back into the game for a while, so I had some time to recuperate from the pain and just deal with it. I tried to work my way through it. I was warming up in the first quarter, warming up in the second quarter, and warming up in the third quarter. I was running down the sideline, trying to do sprints. I started thinking warming up was probably harder than just playing.

Late in the fourth quarter we were driving, and it was time for me to run the football. They put me in the game and gave me a couple of consecutive runs. I broke a run off to the left side, and the leg held up well enough that I was able to pick up a pretty big gain. I felt good that I was able to contribute. After the game was over I was surprised my leg had held up the way it had. I thought it was going to go back to being like spaghetti. But I guess the adrenaline helped me through it and got me through the last couple of plays of the game. In part because of my contributions, Jeff Reed ended up kicking a game-winning field goal. It was a good feeling.

After the game I got the chance to talk with Kordell Stewart. It's always good to see him. I consider him a close friend. Seeing him was meaningful because he got the chance to meet my daughter for the first time. That was pretty cool. I had the opportunity to see his son previously, when he was real young. I was happy to show off my daughter to him. We got a chance to reminisce about the days past and past glories. That is always fun.

We talked about the off-season and the golf bets we were going to have. We talked about how much golfing we were going to do and how much

I was banged up against the Ravens but managed to play through the pain and contribute to an exciting 20–19 win.

money I was going to take from him. He proceeded to tell me how much better he had gotten. He was already a better golfer than I was, but he had gotten better. There was no question that he was going to take all of my money that golf season. I let him know I might have a little surprise for him, that I'll always be one step ahead of him. My golf game had gotten better, too, but I didn't tell him that part. We love to talk golf, which is a common denominator for us.

GAME 7 VS. BALTIMORE, OCTOBER 31, 2005

	1	2	3	4	Score
Baltimore	7	3	0	9	19
Pittsburgh	7	3	7	3	20

A Change in Command

As we were getting ready to play the Packers we learned that Ben Roethlisberger was going to need surgery on his knee. It was a very depressing time. The whole team took a shot in the ribs in the sense that the kid who was now our leader was going to be out, with the possibility of him being out for a while. But he needed the surgery, so there was nothing to do but make the best of it. It's something every team has to deal with.

In came Charlie Batch to replace Ben. The question we all had was, "Can Charlie get it done?" He hadn't played in so long. The one positive was that he had played at Lambeau Field. He was a starter with the Lions, but he never won there. There were a lot of things to consider. But we knew we were going to run the ball and we would be fine if we did that.

For me it was a game in which I needed to be realistic with myself about my injury. I knew if something happened and the team needed me to go in, I wouldn't be able to. I wouldn't be the best option for the team because of my quad. We all talked, and I talked to Dr. Jim Bradley, and we came to the conclusion that the quad needed a couple of weeks to heal and rest. The decision was made for me to sit out of the Green Bay game. I was sitting in the training room, and the prognosis was two or three weeks. The next thing you know Ben comes into the training room with his surgically repaired knee. I looked at him and thought to myself, "Ben's out about three to four weeks. Looks like I am out two to three weeks, and the other guys are going to have to carry the load." That wouldn't necessarily be the case on the field, but off the field someone else would have to encourage the team and get other guys to step it up. They would need someone to challenge them because two of the guys who did that before were laid up in the training room.

On a positive note, the Green Bay game was Duce's first opportunity to play that season. He had knee surgery at the beginning of training camp and had been out pretty much the entire camp and was trying to get healthy again. This was his opportunity to show he was healthy.

Going into the Green Bay game, it became apparent that Ben and I would be out for at least a few games. I knew with Duce Staley coming back we could carry the load on the field, but I worried that we'd just lost two team leaders to the training room at a critical time in the season.

The one disappointing thing I felt was that this would probably be the last time I would get to go to Lambeau Field, which is a pretty historic place. Not being able to play there was a downer.

We got to Green Bay, and not playing is always a difficult thing on the road. You are kind of lazy and you aren't paying a lot of attention. You know you aren't going to be dressing for the game, so you do things slower and with a lot less attention to detail.

Let me tell you, there's not a lot to do in Appleton, Wisconsin. I decided to go to the mall, and it was exactly what I expected. It had a country-western feel to it, including the microbrewery. Not a city environment at all. I got in there and got out. It looked like it could be full of the kind of people who love their Packers so much that the opposing team is their enemy, literally. I went into a hat store and bought a couple of hats. I didn't get any negative comments. I was even asked to sign a Steelers hat, which was cool. I thought it would be a little bit dangerous, but it was harmless. That was a pleasant surprise. But there wasn't much left to the imagination there.

The next day I got to the game and just kind of lingered because I didn't know what to do. I was just trying not to be in anybody's way. In the pregame I was walking around and looking, kind of sightseeing around the stadium. I was trying to get a picture of Lambeau Field from the insider's perspective.

I watched the game from the sideline. Wisconsin on a crisp fall day can be kind of chilly, and I started to get cold. The wind was really whipping. I had to add a towel under my hat because it was so cold. Not playing made it a lot harder. When the game started, the defense rose to the occasion. It was a tough day offensively. The one nice thing was Duce getting the opportunity to pound out some great yardage. He did a great job. Late in the game he scored a touchdown that closed it and sealed the deal. That was fun because Duce is a good friend. To see him succeed was great. I was his biggest cheerleader. When he scored I forgot my quad was hurt. I tried to sprint over to him to congratulate him, until I realized there was some pain and I had to stop. During the game he would ask me if I saw anything, and I'd tell him anything I

GAME 8 AT GREEN BAY, NOVEMBER 6, 2005

	1	2	3	4	Score
Pittsburgh	6	7	0	7	20
Green Bay	3	0	7	0	10

noticed. More important, I let him know he did a great job. I knew he was tired because he hadn't been playing and his lungs were tired. He needed oxygen, and I teased him about that.

Charlie was starting quarterback for the game. There was a lot coming at him in the sense that it was his first opportunity to play in two years. That was significant in terms of seeing the speed of the game. I don't know if the game ever did slow down for him that day. The Packers have some pretty good pass rushers and were putting some pressure on us that day. It made his day tough. The defense saved the day for us, and we got out of there with a win. Brett Favre was his usual self, making plays, but at the end he didn't make enough plays, so we were able to pull it out.

I talked to Brett after the game. He looked good. I told him, "Not bad for us old timers." He told me we have to keep it going. He was trying to get me to think about another year.

STILL A RIVAL,
BUT JUST NOT THE SAME

The next week the Cleveland Browns came to town. It's still a heated rivalry between the two cities, which are only a little more than 100 miles apart, but the Browns aren't our number-one chief rival anymore. It will always be a big game, but the rivalry lost a lot of its luster. When the original Browns moved to Baltimore and became the Ravens, a lot of the hate for the team moved with them. Baltimore is our main rival now. But it's still Cleveland playing against Pittsburgh, and whenever those two teams play it's going to be heated.

In the first half Charlie Batch got hurt, and I felt so sad for him. He was having a good game and led us on a scoring drive. But then he got hurt and had to come out of the game. It was frustrating and sad that he wasn't able to continue what he set out to do.

Tommy Maddox came in to start the second half. I was glad he got another opportunity. The last time he played he didn't have a particularly good day. He took a lot of criticism and heat. Some of it was warranted, some unwarranted. This was a chance for him to exorcise those demons and come out and win the football game. He went out there and on the first play threw an interception, but fortunately it was called back. He got a reprieve and breathed a huge sigh of relief. Most people don't get that lucky, but he did. He was able to go out there and finish the game, and we won the football game. I was happy Tommy was able to get back in there and get things going.

Charlie Batch held his own under some intense pressure from the Packers, and that's no small feat after sitting on the sideline for an entire two seasons. *Photo courtesy of AP/Wide World Photos.*

Brett Favre could only watch as Troy Polamalu returned a fumble 77 yards for a touchdown. But with Brett's competitive spirit, all he wanted to talk about after the game was the two of us sticking it out for another year. *Photo courtesy of AP/Wide World Photos.*

FRUSTRATION IN BALTIMORE

The following week Tommy started the game against Baltimore, and we knew it was going to be a physical game. The one thing we didn't factor in was that Trai Essex was going to have to start in place of Marvel Smith. We didn't know the impact that would have. Baltimore, having played us and knowing Tommy's weaknesses, put a lot of pressure on him and got his feet moving and created disruption. They were pretty successful. They were able to stop the running game and make us pretty one-dimensional. They got after Tommy a lot. Our defense kept us in the game, but we weren't able to do anything offensively. Not until the last quarter were we finally able to drive the ball down there and score.

BETTIS ON THE MEDIA

The quarterback situation and the injuries quite naturally got a huge amount of attention in Pittsburgh. It amazed me when regular programming on TV was broken into to give an update on Ben Roethlisberger and his knee injury. This told me it was not just sports, it was news. It was actually breaking news for the people of Pittsburgh. It was like something with the president. It takes a lot to break into regularly scheduled programming to give an update. For them to do that it told me they are really, really serious about their Steelers, and number one is the quarterback. For the news to do that you know it's a pretty significant situation. As a player you don't think what you do is that significant. Obviously the public feels differently.

I couldn't help but notice the extra media in the locker room. I saw people I wouldn't normally see, people who cover different types of stories—news stories—and I had to wonder what they were doing there.

I realized that this was being covered not just as a sports story but as a news-related story. It was weird to see.

GAME 9 VS. CLEVELAND, NOVEMBER 13, 2005

	1	2	3	4	Score
Cleveland	7	0	0	14	21
Pittsburgh	0	17	7	10	34

Charlie is congratulated after a touchdown against the rival Browns in the second quarter, but he soon would get knocked out of the game. *Photo courtesy of AP/Wide World Photos.*

GAME 10 AT BALTIMORE, NOVEMBER 20, 2005

	1	2	3	4	OT	Score
Pittsburgh	0	6	0	7	0	13
Baltimore	0	13	0	0	3	16

The Ravens had been leading the entire game. It was one of those games in which you knew maybe the last team with the ball would win the game. They were blitzing and getting after us. They got a lot of pressure on Tommy and sacked him quite a few times. They tried to take advantage of Trai being a rookie left tackle. It was discouraging the way the offense played because we didn't play as well as we were capable of playing. That was frustrating, really frustrating. They were able to take advantage of that. Their offense isn't that potent, and we were able to contain them for the most part. We scored, tied the game up, and sent it into overtime.

In overtime we felt pretty good. The last couple of series in regulation we were able to move the ball down and score, so we felt good about getting the football. We started driving but had to punt the ball away. I was thinking the defense had been playing well, so we'd get good field position, get the ball back, and score. And the defense did hold them and forced them to punt to us. We were driving and moving the ball downfield when we became the victim of one of those fluke plays that you either love or hate, depending on which side you're rooting for. Tommy threw it to Hines, but the ball was batted around as Hines made a desperate leap to try to grab it. As he jumped for it, he kicked it in the air, and Terrell Suggs made an incredible grab. It was reviewed, and though I still don't think it was a catch, it was ruled an interception. The Ravens marched down the field and kicked a game-winning field goal.

In the Ravens game we passed the ball a lot. I really think that as a team—coaching staff and players alike—we didn't believe we could run the football in that game. This became obvious in one particular situation, when on fourth-and-one we threw the football instead of running it, which is what we live and die by. If you stop us on a run, so be it. But if you stop us on a pass play and sack us in the bargain, we aren't playing our best game. I think the lack of the running game did us in. I knew we didn't run the ball much, so I was wondering what was going on. In fairness, I would have to say that our running game wasn't all that effective that day, but we weren't doing any better throwing the ball because we weren't giving Tommy much protection. But still, our offense is geared to the run, and we get ourselves into trouble when we get away from our running game. We are a running football team, and if we can't run, we don't have a chance.

Tommy Maddox was under a lot of pressure from that great Baltimore defense all day, but he still helped us get into an overtime situation. We just came up short in a 16–13 final.

It was frustrating because the Ravens game was a game we should have won. We knew they were going to play us tough, but we didn't expect to lose. The reality set in that we had dug ourselves into a pretty deep hole with the undefeated Colts up next on the schedule. We were chasing Cincinnati because they got off to such a good start. We knew we had just given away a game that, in the scheme of things, we knew we had to win. Whenever you lose a football game, you know it can come back to haunt you. That loss, along with Jacksonville, are two games you look at yourself and say, those are two games we should have won. You kick yourself because that might be the reason you don't make it to the playoffs.

When you get home from a game like that you try to block it out of your mind. In this case it wasn't so hard to do because we knew we had to face the league-leading Colts the following week. But the nasty taste of a loss was there, and it gave us a negative feel in the locker room going into the next game.

REFLECTIONS IN THE REARVIEW MIRROR

Here I am posing in my Mackenzie High School uniform at the age of 18 and pounding away for yardage with three Finney High defenders along for the ride.

Photos courtesy of the Bettis family.

6

No Monday Night Party

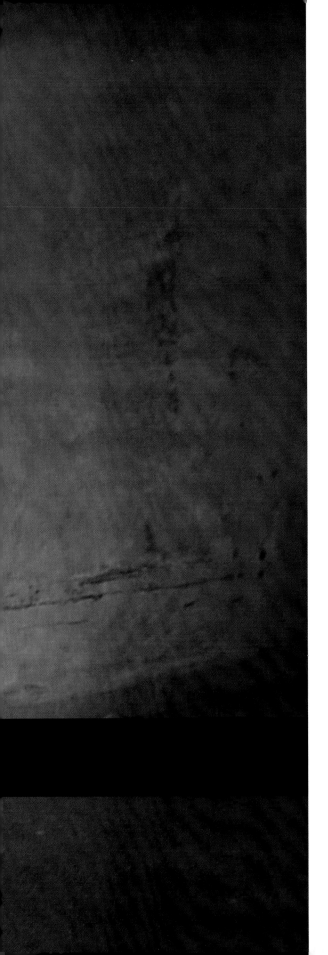

We all knew the Colts game was going to be a tough challenge, but we were up for it. We planned to reestablish the running game and were going to run it down their throats. We felt we had an equalizer. But we were very, very wrong in that regard.

We felt good, though. Marvel Smith was coming back to go against the Colts' Dwight Freeney, one of the best pass rushers in the game. Our defense a couple of years ago stopped Peyton Manning and figured him out. We felt good about our chances against the Colts.

Marvel went out of the game in the first quarter with an ankle injury, and Trai came in. It didn't hurt us that much. Freeney was giving it to us with or without Marvel in the game. He was an animal out there. He was creating havoc. He wasn't necessarily getting to the quarterback, but he was creating enough disruption that it was hard for us to do much of anything offensively.

That game was very disappointing. On their first play from scrimmage, Manning hit Marvin Harrison on an 80-yard touchdown bomb, and it didn't get any better for us after that. We went out there on *Monday Night Football* in front of a huge national audience and laid an egg. Offensively we couldn't throw the football, we couldn't run the football. Nothing we did seemed to work. It looked as though they had figured out everything we tried, and they just flat-out outplayed us. It was disappointing because we had never been on as big a stage as *Monday Night Football* and not played well. That was frustrating, but to their credit, the Colts caused us not to play well.

Ben came back in the game against the Colts. He didn't seem that rusty, but I don't think he had a lot of time to make plays. He was able to escape the rush some of the time. For the most part he didn't get a lot of time to do much. The offensive line wasn't able to handle the Colts' defensive front. As a result, Ben took a beating both in the pocket and when he tried to run.

In the second half of the game we started with an onside kick. I thought it was ill-advised because we had stopped them in the second quarter, though giving them a field goal late because of an interception. Defensively we were doing a good job and not letting them march down the football field. I felt the defense could hold them when we kicked off to them. If we did, and then scored when we got the ball back, we would be down only two points. But the onside kick gave them a short field, and when they scored a touchdown on third down, it was demoralizing.

When you do an onside kick you're as much as telling the other team that you're not sure your defense can stop them. It sends a little message to the other team that you need to try a little trickery to beat them and get the ball back. That's the wrong message to send. They were a lot smarter than we were, and they were ready for us.

We knew that third touchdown was a momentum swing. It put the fans back in the game for the Colts, and that was one thing we couldn't afford.

That crowd was incredible. The noise was deafening. It created an incredible home-field advantage. The noise and the pass rushers that they have make it almost impossible for an offense to be consistent up and down the field. We heard a lot about them pumping the crowd noise in. I am willing to bet if they didn't pump it in it would still be loud enough to the point where you couldn't hear or have your offense function. Maybe, maybe not. But with the team they have, it probably wouldn't make a lot of difference.

A LETDOWN AT HOME

Coming back from a Monday night game is tiring. You don't have time to recuperate the way you would like to. It's very demanding, and it's especially tough when your body gets beat up. It's asking a lot to be ready. Having an opponent like Cincinnati coming up, a critical game you just can't lose because then you go two down to the division leader, makes it doubly tough. It becomes a must-win. If we ever had a must-win game in the 2005 season, it was December 4 against Cincinnati.

Going into the game we knew we had run into a buzz saw in Indianapolis the week before, and we had to get back on track. We felt we matched up well against the Bengals running the football. Plus, they hadn't beaten us in a while and we were playing at home. We were feeling good about what we thought we could do.

We didn't have a team meeting or any cause for concern. We just knew we had to keep focus. We knew we had dug ourselves a hole and had to get out of it, and we were hoping this was the game to do it. Everybody understood the gravity of this game and what it meant. We felt good getting ready for it.

The Monday night game against the Colts was a huge disappointment. On their first play from scrimmage, Marvin Harrison broke free for an 80-yard TD reception, and things never looked up for us. *Photo courtesy of AP/Wide World Photos.*

GAME 11 AT INDIANAPOLIS, NOVEMBER 28, 2005

	1	2	3	4	Score
Pittsburgh	7	0	0	0	7
Indianapolis	10	6	7	3	26

Guys like Chad Johnson of the Bengals talked a little trash before the game, but we didn't pay that much attention to it. We were determined about one thing, however, and that was to not let him score. We didn't want him doing his little routine in our end zones at Heinz Field. So that was our goal: keep Johnson out of the end zone.

The game itself proved frustrating. Everything that could go wrong did go wrong. We fumbled the football two or three times. We were intercepted. We did not handle their pressure well, and they came out pretty much on fire. They did everything right. But through the course of the game, even though we could never really catch up, we were never really out of it. Late in the game we had an opportunity to close the gap.

The crowd noise at Indy was incredible. Their fans create a major home-field advantage, but this one was wrong about who would be going to the **Super Bowl.** *Photo courtesy of AP/Wide World Photos.*

Down a touchdown, we got the ball back and thought we had a really good chance to take it down the field and score, but it was not to be, unfortunately, and we lost the football game.

Losing that game made our situation pretty desperate. We were down two games and in all probability no longer had much of a shot at winning our division. This had been a big game, and we lost an opportunity to win our division for the first time in I don't know how many years. There was a small panic that went through everybody. We understood now that in order for us to get into the playoffs, we were going to have to win every game from there on out and we were going to need some help. We were in a bad situation.

It was a hard pill to swallow because we weren't able to run the football against the Bengals. I don't think it was because of their defense especially. It was our own lack of execution. We didn't sustain drives on third down. We didn't complete third-down plays to stay on field. We turned the ball over. We didn't give ourselves a chance to be the offense that we can be. That was the frustrating part.

The one good thing that came out of that game was that Ben was able to throw the ball well, the offense opened up, and he had a really strong game. It gave him the confidence he needed, and it gave the coaching staff the confidence of knowing that if we needed to throw the football that we would be okay. I think some good did come out of the game, but obviously it was more bad than good. I think for the first time we became a team that was really unsure of itself, and that was the scary part. We didn't really know if we could rebound from such a devastating loss.

THE MORNING AFTER

That Monday everyone was in a very somber mood. In fact, I'd say the mood was pretty ugly. I think some self-doubt started to seep in. In the team meeting Coach Cowher asked us to look at ourselves first before we started pointing fingers at someone else or jumping to conclusions about how someone else played. He told us to look at the film and grade ourselves on each and every play, on technique, on assignments, and on effort. If you do that first you get a true understanding of where you are and you won't be so fast to criticize the next guy. It also gave each man a chance to accurately assess his strengths and weaknesses. Sometimes you get a false sense of reality, and when you don't win, or even when you do win, you think you are playing better than you are. This gave everyone a chance to look at himself closely and gauge his performance. It gave everyone the understanding that if we are going to win and go forward, every man has to do his part and play his role.

Then we returned home and dropped a second straight game, a critical loss to the Bengals. Our offense looked better against the Bengals than it did in Indy, and I got the scoring started in the first quarter, but it was a devastating loss.

GAME 12 VS. CINCINNATI, DECEMBER 4, 2005

	1	2	3	4	Score
Cincinnati	7	14	10	7	38
Pittsburgh	14	3	7	7	31

The Fox network chose the Monday after the Cincinnati game to tape a piece called *The Day After*: what it takes to get the Bus started the morning after a game.

It was great that we were able to look at ourselves because then nobody would cast the first stone. That was the point where everyone came to the recognition that if we want to do it, we have to do it ourselves and it's going to take every man to make a concerted effort.

Unfortunately for me there were not a lot of plays that I was in on, and when I was in, I honestly thought I put forth my best effort. I scored a touchdown and was pleased with my overall performance.

Jay Glazer, a good friend of mine who works for the Fox network, asked me to do a piece with him based on how I feel the Monday after. They picked the Monday after the Cincinnati game. It was frustrating because we lost, and that always makes it worse. Glazer asked if his crew could be there when I woke up on Monday, so I said okay. They filmed me just doing my normal daily routine on a Monday. They got me getting up and going, having breakfast; they got me stretching, riding the bike, the whole routine of getting the legs moving. They got me in the sauna and then heading into work. They followed me in the training room, too. I got a massage one night they were there. They were around quite a bit that week. But it was good.

Having the crew there wasn't too intrusive on my daily activities. It wasn't that bad in the sense of being too open. I think the piece gave everyone outside of the organization the opportunity to see what a day in the life of the Bus is like and what I go through on a daily basis. People can then appreciate more what you have to do because of what you go through. I think it was good.

REFLECTIONS IN THE REARVIEW MIRROR

At age 16 I was called upon to host a prom (not my own); and below, of course, is my graduation photo from Mackenzie High, where I graduated with honors. *Photos courtesy of the Bettis family.*

7 Our Playoffs Have Started

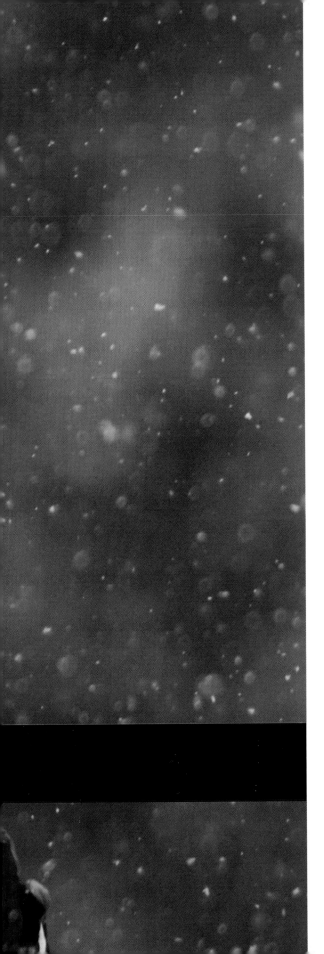

The team had a meeting the Wednesday after
the Bengals game. Our goal board is in the front of the team meeting
room. Usually we have the whole season of games on the board and you
have how well you did in them based on certain categories. Coach had
wiped all of the other games off and just had Chicago, our next opponent,
written up there. It really emphasized the fact that it's just one game. This
is the season. He was able to capture the moment. Everyone was looking
up there and seeing just one game. It let us know that if we didn't win this
game, nothing else mattered. Basically we didn't have any more games.
That was the only one; if we lost we were going home.

Our playoffs started a lot earlier than most in the sense that every game
after the Cincinnati game became a playoff game. I think it was good for us.
It focused everybody. Everybody understood that it was make or break.

The way that Coach got it across to us, it was very clear what needed to
be done. There was no rally cry or anything like that, no rah-rah, just
a bunch of men going about their business and knowing what needed to
be done. We all understood what was at stake. This is a veteran football
team. Everybody understood what it meant. Going out and practicing
those first couple of days we were very spirited.

The Chicago Bears were the team standing in our way. They were a
good football team, but we felt we had to win. We didn't have a choice.

The game plan for the Bears game didn't say a whole lot. The one thing
Coach Cowher told me was to be ready early. He told me this is my type
of game. But there was nothing out of the ordinary that would lead me
to believe that my role would be any different or greater. On the basis of
the game plan, nothing indicated my role would change at all.

The game was a must-win for us. We were playing a first-place team that
had really destroyed a lot of good football teams. It was a game we were
very cautious of. We had some success early, and we thought we were
going to be okay because we thought their offense wasn't going to be

The Bears game was a must-win situation for us, and despite the poor weather conditions we were able to stick to our game plan and get our season back on track. *Photo courtesy of AP/Wide World Photos.*

	1	2	3	4	Score
Chicago	3	0	0	6	9
Pittsburgh	7	7	7	0	21

able to score too many points on our defense. As the game unfolded we were able to get on top of them early, and our defense was able to handle their offense and stop them on their first drive down in the red zone. It was a big drive, and they only got a field goal. We came back and pounded on them again, and then the weather started to change in the second quarter and I was able to score on a one-yard run.

By the third quarter, the weather really started to get bad. It was starting to get snowy. I was able to score another touchdown. That was a fun one because I had the chance to run over a couple of guys doing it, one key guy being Brian Urlacher. It was fun because I had never played against Urlacher. It was one of those times when I thought, "Okay, let's see what he's made of." To get an opportunity to get in the end zone through him was fun.

Throughout the game the weather kept getting snowier and more out of control. As more snow fell, I knew the ground was going to get ugly. At that point I knew my number was going to be called. That is my forte: playing games in bad weather. I knew the opportunity was going to come, and sure enough they called my number. I started to go to work, and play after play everything started to really come through. I was running physical and strong. I got a chance to break one, and that was fun. It was a 39-yard run, and I kind of tripped up and ended up going out of bounds. On the sideline all of the quarterbacks were standing together, and I saw them all looking at me and talking and looking back at me. Ben asked me to come over, and I did. Ben said, "If you hadn't tripped, do you think you would have scored?" Immediately Tommy Maddox busted out laughing, and Charlie Batch was laughing. I said very seriously, "No, I definitely would have scored." At that point they erupted again. I even started laughing. That was a funny moment.

The game turned out a lot different from what I expected at the beginning. I didn't expect to have that much of an impact. As the game wore on and they gave me carry after carry, before I knew it I was approaching 100 yards and we were getting close to the end of the game at the same time. On the last play I was in on, I thought I had just 100 yards, so I was saying to myself, "Just don't get thrown for a loss." And what happens? Of course, as soon as I get the ball this guy hits me and, boom,

I've always thrived in bad weather conditions, and I was able to get into the end zone again in the Chicago game.

I lose a yard. I'm thinking to myself that I just lost the 100-yard game I had worked so hard for. Luckily for me I was still just over 100 and didn't lose it. I ended up with 101 yards. That was funny, and a relief.

Some people have the impression that I love playing in bad weather, but that's misleading. I think because I've had some success in bad weather a lot of people just assume that I enjoy it, but I don't. It's terrible weather, and it's terrible for me because it's wet and nasty. But I am consistent in those conditions, so it doesn't affect me in some of the ways it affects the other guys. It's not that I play great in it, it just doesn't affect me as much as it does other players. Maybe it has something to do with my body type and the fact that I sink into the mud a little bit more. Some of the other guys glide on top of it. I certainly don't look forward to playing in the mud, or the rain, or the snow, but when I have to play in those conditions, I am just as reliable as when it's dry. I think that is the benefit that I have in a situation like that.

It was surprising for me after the game because most games when I have 100 yards, I am pretty sore. But this time I wasn't really sore because it wasn't a superphysical football game. Some games are physical and smashmouth, but this wasn't one of them. This was one of those games that I was kind of cutting through there like a hot knife through butter, so thankfully I wasn't too sore afterward. It felt good. Maybe I did get the illusion that I could do it every week, but that went away in a hurry once I got to practice.

ANOTHER MUST-WIN UPON US

Coming back we had to play the Minnesota Vikings on the road. I missed practice on Wednesday because I hurt my quad in the Chicago game. That was frustrating because I was running well, but I kept getting it banged up. I took Wednesday off, and on Thursday I went limited. Friday I started to feel better with the quad. I was concerned that if I got hit on it before the game that it would be a bad thing. I was extra cautious that week with my injury. I had a big old pad on it to make sure nobody hit it. It was scary, but I was able to get through it.

Going into Minnesota we were the underdogs. Sometimes you like being in the underdog role, but we didn't really like it because we had to win. If the game doesn't really matter, win or lose, then yeah, it's great to be the underdog. But when you have to win, you want to be the favorite and the other team to be struggling. We were facing a team on a six-game winning streak, and they had found ways to win every week whether it was defense, special teams, or offense. We knew this team was capable of beating us, so it was just a matter of us going out there and playing our style of game, and playing for 60 minutes. We knew it was going to be difficult because they had a different set of obstacles for us compared to the Bears, but we still felt we could win. The Bears defense was fast, but they weren't big up front. This group was big up front, with really talented guys in the front seven. They had big linebackers. We knew it was going to be a lot harder based on our style of play.

We knew it was going to be difficult for us to run the football, and we knew the crowd was going to play a part. We practiced all week with the crowd noise and the silent snap so that we didn't go through the same mistakes that we went through in Indianapolis in terms of not being able to hear and communicate. We learned our lesson there and put some different things into play to try to combat that. That was a good thing.

When the game started it was loud and the fans were energized. It was a seesaw game early on. It was one of those games that our defense just refused to let anything bad happen to us. We made mistake after mistake offensively, and they bailed us out. We had a fumble on a punt return, and they limited them to three points. They kept us in the game and gave us the opportunity to really stretch our lead out. That game was definitely one of those games in which the defense took over and gave us every chance to win.

One good thing was that we had a lot of fans there, and they were making a lot of noise, too. It didn't surprise me because everywhere we go we draw so many fans and we have such great support on the road. It is phenomenal. I can look back year after year and point to games where our fans almost outnumbered the home team's fans. Year after year you think you just saw an anomaly, something that really could never happen with the fans, and then the next year the fans do something on an even grander scale. The fan support was just incredible. To their credit they made it difficult on the home team, and that was great to see. I love that our fans give us that kind of support and that they are that smart to understand that we are the road team but they still can create an advantage for us by being loud. That was great. It is great to have such knowledgeable fans who know they can make a difference.

GAME 14 AT MINNESOTA, DECEMBER 18, 2005

	1	2	3	4	Score
Pittsburgh	3	7	6	2	18
Minnesota	3	0	0	0	3

It was frustrating to be banged up again going into the Vikings game because I'd been running well the previous two weeks, but I was able to help the team and keep our playoff hopes alive.

THE GRINCH THAT STOLE CHRISTMAS FROM CLEVELAND

Our next mission was Cleveland on Christmas Eve. It's not hard staying up for these must-win games, even against a team that didn't have a good record. We knew if we lost we were going home. It's one of those situations that if you know what you want, it's right in front of you and yours for the taking. If you are willing to sacrifice and go get it, it's there. The knowledge that only if we kept winning could our season keep going was all the motivation we needed. It wasn't a problem trying to motivate ourselves because we understood if we lost, we'd be done. We had no illusions. The question was whether we could do the things we needed to do to win. That was the question on everyone's mind.

The approach going into Cleveland was, like the last couple of games, that it was an absolutely must-win situation. Cleveland, of course, wanted to win as well, but it was more important to us than it was to them, so we had to come out there with more intensity than they had and show them that we needed this game more than they did. That was the thought going into Cleveland. They are our rivals, it's Pittsburgh-Cleveland, but this was a road playoff game for us, and that was the mentality we were going to have. We were focused and ready. We had to play solid defense, run the ball well, and have good special-teams play. That is the recipe for success in the playoffs, and that's what we wanted to do. Nobody even had an inkling that we would lose that football game. Everyone felt supreme confidence, and I think it showed as we got out there and played.

The week of the game there was some sad news in the NFL. James Dungy, the son of Colts head coach Tony Dungy, was found dead. It hit me hard, especially because I am a father now and I understand the loss of a child. Just the thought of that and how devastating it would be seems almost too much to bear. I know how important my daughter is to me. To have someone in our fraternity, in our family, lose a child like that was the most devastating thing in the world. Our hearts went out to him and his family. We said prayers for them that they might be given strength to cope, to come to some understanding of that terrible and unanswerable question of why. It's very disturbing. My heart just went out to them.

You understand that you can go from the best year of your life in terms of football to the worst year of your life. That is what Coach Dungy went through. He was having the best year from a team standpoint, and then tragedy struck and turned his world upside down. It shows you that this is just a game and there are things in life that are a lot more important. It gives new understanding and perspective, a reminder not to take the game that seriously because at the end of the day, it's still a game.

We ran up against another physical defense in Cleveland, but we needed the win more than the Browns did, and everything seemed to go our way.

We were fired up for the Browns and treated it as a playoff game, but the 41–0 blowout was more than we could have expected, even on Christmas Eve.

GAME 15 AT CLEVELAND, DECEMBER 24, 2005

	1	2	3	4	Score
Pittsburgh	14	6	14	7	41
Cleveland	0	0	0	0	0

OUR PLAYOFFS HAVE STARTED

BETTIS ON FAMILY

It's hard to put into words the fulfillment you get and the joy you have when you have a child. We lost the AFC Championship game in 2005, and the next week my daughter was born. She took away all of the pain and anguish of a tough season just with her presence. When she arrived, it was a burst of energy and joy all balled up into one little person. She stole my heart. She has been a blessing in my life and has given me a reason to keep going.

My wife, Trameka, was never really that knowledgeable about football until we started dating. It wasn't that important to her, in the scheme of things, until then. As our relationship developed, her knowledge of the game developed. It's funny to see, now that she is a fan and knows what is going on. After the games we always had a critique session. She would tell me about the game from her perspective. It was a fun part of her learning process for us to talk about my performance. She became my biggest critic throughout the years. She has always been there for me. Regardless of what I wanted to do, she has been there for me 100 percent.

My parents have been there for every game that I have played. They only missed two preseason games, one in Mexico and one in Japan. They have been my security blanket. They have always been there, win, lose, or draw. It's all about them loving their son, and that's what I enjoy. They show their love for me by being there for me. When I stepped on the football field it meant a lot just knowing they were there to give me a kiss and let me know they love me no matter what happened in the game. It gave me more of a burst knowing they were there to watch me, and I never wanted to let them down. They were my biggest fans.

I don't know what they are going to do this fall now that football is over. They have been so much a part of my career. They have become huge football fans, and I don't know if they can just turn the switch off. It's going to be hard for me to be away from football, but I think it's going to be equally difficult for them because they have been around football for as long as I have.

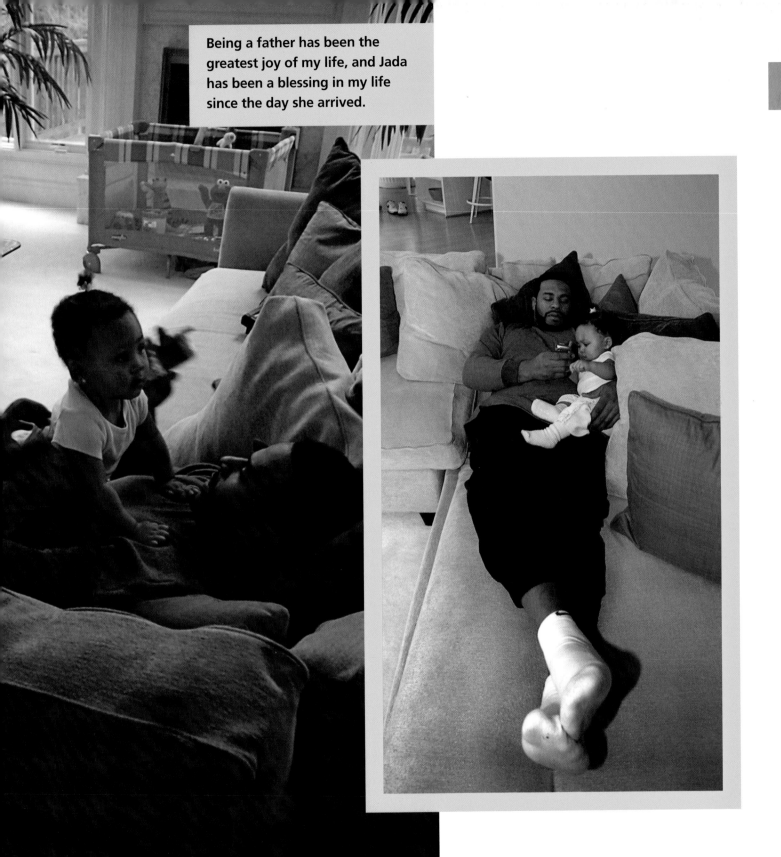

Being a father has been the greatest joy of my life, and Jada has been a blessing in my life since the day she arrived.

It was a treat for Trameka and me to be able to introduce Jada to the team and to have my teammates see me in the role of a father for the first time.

We knew we had a good chance to win because we were going against a rookie quarterback. Our defense does very well against rookie quarterbacks because of the different looks we give, the movement, the blitzing, and all of the pressure we're able to bring. We can make things pretty tough on rookie quarterbacks. We knew that it was going to be hard for their offense to try to sustain drives. We knew it was more important for us to try to get after them offensively. They had a good defense in the sense that they didn't give up a lot of big plays. They were ranked decently in the league in total defense. We knew they were a good defensive team and that we would have to put together some good drives to really take control of the game. We knew it was going to be a dogfight, and we certainly didn't think it would be a 41–0 blowout.

The game ended with a hit that preserved the shutout. Larry Foote hit Browns player Aaron Shea and stopped him short of the end zone. That game gave us an enormous amount of confidence because we were able to keep a team out of the end zone for a complete game. That's impressive. To stop that team every single time and then put the exclamation point at the end, that was fun to see. Larry and Shea went to college together, and for Larry to clean Shea's clock like that was fun. It showed that our bond as teammates is thicker than the bond they had as teammates in college.

It was especially fun because it was Cleveland. Whenever you can beat up on Cleveland it's fun. Also the fact that we had to win the game and we did. It's Cleveland versus Pittsburgh, and to blow them out at their place was really special. The fans were yelling and screaming and booing us, and we just annihilated them. It was fun to see their fans piling out of that stadium with a sick look on their faces. We were the Grinch that stole Christmas, and that was great.

There was an incident in the game when a fan ran out onto the field. I was kind of nervous at first because I didn't know what this guy was trying to do, but he was running toward Verron Haynes. It was one of those things where you don't know what the guy's intentions are. It was scary to a degree. Then James Harrison got hold of him. Harrison brought the fan down to the ground, and it kind of defused things quite nicely. It was a WWF-style takedown. One thing I will say is that I doubt that fan will do that again. When the man first ran at Verron, Verron kind of ran away from him a little bit. He had a free opportunity to protect himself. We got on Verron pretty good on the sideline, and he took a beating for that. He lost a lot of street credibility for that one. If he had defended himself a little better than that he would have won over a lot of support. I didn't say anything to James. He seemed like he was in a zone, so I wanted to leave him there. I didn't want to be the next guy to go down like that.

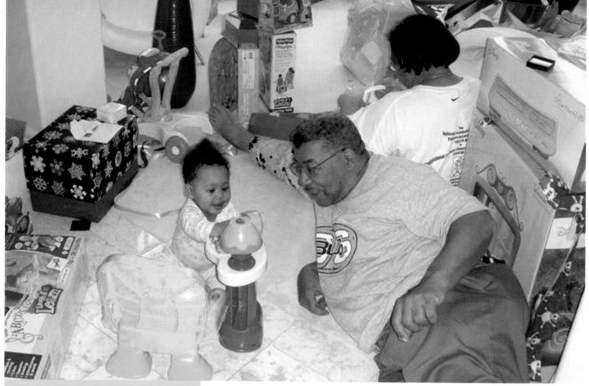

It was really special to be able to spend Jada's first Christmas with my folks in Pittsburgh. She had a ball, but I think they had even more fun.

JADA'S FIRST CHRISTMAS

In December we had the chance to take my daughter, Jada, to the team's Christmas party. It was a lot of fun because everyone from the office wanted to see her. They had seen pictures of her, but not too many people had met her in person. I can tell you she was the star of the party. It was quite an introduction. Everyone wanted to hold her and play with her. She was 10 months old at the time and as cute as she could be. It was great that Trameka and I were able to bring her. She is such a good baby. She is not a crier or anything like that. She goes to people; she is not too shy. It was great because everyone got a chance to see my joy. That was an incredible feeling.

I was proud. This is my first child. I have been on this team so long and everybody knows me on a personal level, but they got to see me as a father, and to see my daughter, which made me really proud because she is the light of my life. To be able to share that and let everyone meet her was special. It was fun, it really was. She usually just sees me and Mommy at home. For her to get out and see everybody was a treat for her, too. It wasn't just everybody meeting her; it was her meeting everybody who is important in my life as well.

She also got a chance to see Santa for the first time. We took a lot of pictures, and that was a highlight. I wasn't worried how she would do seeing Santa. She never cries unless Daddy does something wrong. I knew she would be good, but I was afraid Santa's beard might be a problem. We decided to back her into Santa's lap instead of just giving her to Santa because I knew once she looked up and saw this guy with all of that scary white hair that the jig was going to be up. It was imperative that we get those pictures quick.

I didn't have to do any Christmas shopping. I'm not a shopper, but fortunately Trameka doesn't mind, and she did all of the shopping. She is great at that. She got all of the kids' gifts, gifts for family and friends, and gifts for all of the nieces and nephews. She did all of the hard work, and I was able to just concentrate on football.

We spent Christmas morning in Pittsburgh. Cleveland is halfway between Detroit and Pittsburgh, so my mother, father, and sister came to the game against the Browns on Christmas Eve, and then they drove to Pittsburgh and had Christmas in Pittsburgh with us. That was great to have my mother and father spend Christmas with their granddaughter. That was fun. It was my first Christmas as a father. For them to be able to be there and have us all celebrate Christmas together made it very memorable.

We woke up early Christmas morning and couldn't wait to take Jada downstairs. She got to see the tree and all of the gifts. She was really tearing those gifts open. At some point she was more interested in the paper than she was in the gifts. We had to just give her the presents. She had a ball. It was her day. We just let her do what she wanted and play with all of her toys. Toys were all over the house, but it was okay because it was Christmas.

We held back a little bit on the gifts. You don't want to do too much because at some point it is overkill. Plus, her birthday is at the end of January, and we knew we'd be doing it all over again in a month. We did it big, but we didn't overdo it.

My mother, father, and sister were going to be driving back to Detroit before dinner, so we decided to have Christmas brunch as a family. My father and Trameka cooked breakfast. They made everything: grits, bacon, sausage, eggs, pancakes, waffles, and cinnamon bread. It was great being able to do that with the family. There was so much food that I ate twice.

It was nice to have a game on Christmas Eve and then not have to work at all on Christmas Day. A lot of past years we have had to work on Christmas. We would get the morning off, but we would still have to come in to work. We wouldn't get the opportunity to spend the day with the family and enjoy the day. That is the rough part sometimes. But it was a blessing we had this year to be able to get home early enough to have Christmas Eve together and then have Christmas Day together as well. That was fun. I was thankful that the schedule makers decided we should play on Saturday and not on Sunday.

REFLECTIONS IN THE REARVIEW MIRROR

Here's another high school graduation photo (above), along with a family shot (below) with (back row, from left) my dad, cousins Jaron and Jason, friend Ryan, and (front, from left) me, grandfather John Bettis, brother John, and my best friend, Jahmal Dokes. *Photos courtesy of the Bettis family.*

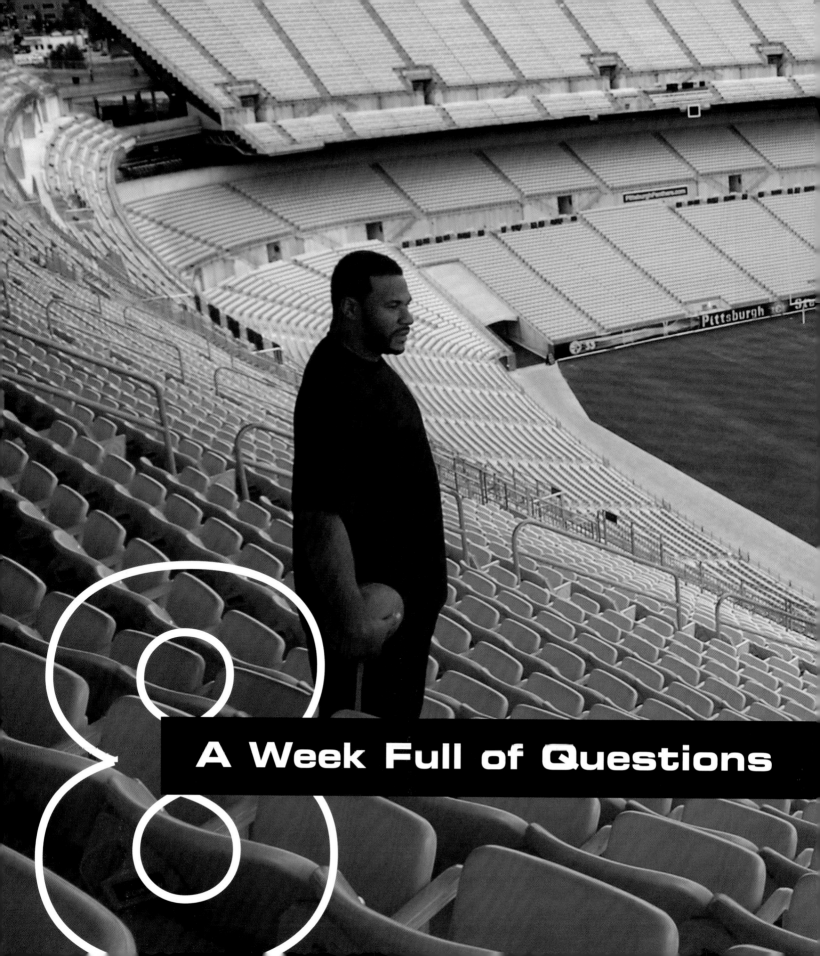

A Week Full of Questions

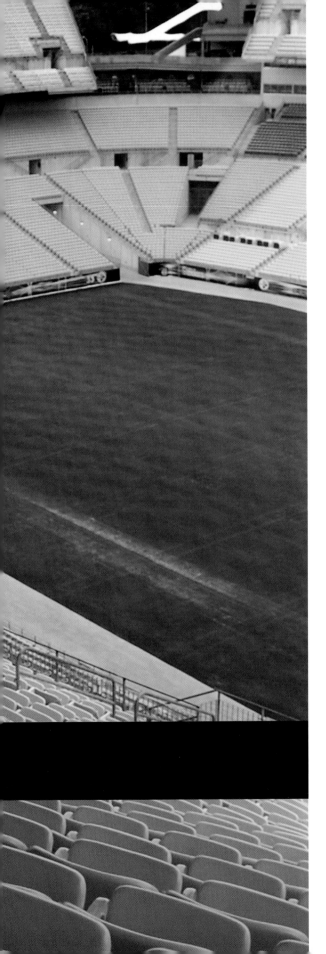

On the Monday before the Lions game, the
final game of the regular season, I started thinking that this might
possibly be my last game ever. It was clear that it could be the last time
I took the field in front of the home crowd. It was a scary thought in
the sense that there wouldn't be any more Sundays in Pittsburgh. I have
had so much success, and playing for the Steelers has been such a big
part of my life that coming up on what could be the last game was a little
frightening.

I anticipated that the media would be asking me about my plans for the
future a lot during the week, so I was trying to decide how I'd answer
the inevitable questions when I wasn't sure what the answer was. All
I was sure of was that I really didn't have an answer. That was my
dilemma, to try to answer questions without lying or even misleading,
but trying to be honest about how I really felt. It was a catch-22. I
wanted to tell them everything, but I didn't know if people were going
to draw the wrong conclusions and print things that would lead to
greater confusion. I decided to take it question by question and walk the
tightrope as best I could.

It made me think about some of the memories. I will never forget the
game at Heinz Field when we played the Jets and all of the Terrible
Towels were waving in unison. It was amazing. I never saw anything
like that before in my life. It was breathtaking. It was awesome to see.

Heinz Field is a great place to play, but I don't think the effect was quite
the same as it was at Three Rivers Stadium. Part of it is because Heinz
is open, which means the noise isn't anywhere near as loud. It's also
different because Three Rivers had a certain ambiance about it. All of
the great ones had gone through there. The one thing we all said when
Heinz Field opened was that we had to create the ambiance, the legacy
and history with our teams. I think it is getting there. I think the fans
realize they have to do a little bit more. It's not as loud, so the fans have
to be louder, and they are doing that. We are giving them more to yell

The week leading up to the Detroit game was filled with media requests and interviews with the same question on everybody's mind: would it be my final game in Pittsburgh?

about, and the stadium is starting to build up that character that Three Rivers had.

That Monday before the Lions game was a pretty normal Monday. There wasn't anything out of the ordinary at the radio show. All season long the kids had been asking questions about whether I was coming back or not, so that wasn't strange in any way. There was a larger than normal crowd. There was a pretty big following for a radio show. That's big. I am there for only half an hour. For the people to come out the way they have and support me has been incredible. Each week has gotten bigger and bigger. This week was no exception. There was an enormous crowd there. It was nothing unusual. It was a good day.

On Tuesday I started to get requests for interviews about what could be the final home game for me. People had tried to get in touch with me on Monday, but I was conveniently unavailable. On Tuesday I gave Ed Bouchette a call. He had been calling me a lot, so I decided on Tuesday to call him back. He is a beat writer for the *Pittsburgh Post-Gazette*. He wanted to do a story about this possibly being my last game at Heinz Field. I was as honest as I could be in terms of not knowing exactly what I was going to do, but I told him what I could. The interview came out pretty well.

When I got to work on Wednesday people told me it was a good article. I read the article, and I knew then it was going to spark a lot of thought from everybody—from my teammates to the coaches to the fans—in terms of the reality of it possibly being my last game at Heinz Field.

During the lunch break that day I was purposely missing from the media because I just didn't want to deal with the questions. I came in after practice and was bombarded by the reporters wanting to know more about the decision. To the best of my ability I tried to explain what I was thinking, what decisions I had to make, and what the basis of my decision would be as far as coming back or not. I went through that, and it wasn't too bad.

Each Wednesday I do a spot on the news on KDKA-TV. The questions that Wednesday were all about whether I was going to stay or not. Ever since the article had come out, that's all anybody wanted to talk about.

A lot of teammates had been coming in with jerseys and pictures and things of that nature for me to sign. I told them, "Hey, I'm not gone yet!" I guess they just wanted to make sure they had pieces of memorabilia, and it made me feel good that I had the respect of my teammates to the point that they wanted to get items signed or pictures taken for keepsakes. That is a big honor to be appreciated in such a way. Not one guy, though, asked me what I was going to do, and I really appreciated that. It's hard enough when the camera is in your face, or when you are on the street or in a restaurant and people are asking you what you are going to do. You get bombarded with questions. The one sanctuary I had was the locker room. The guys didn't ask me. They kind of let me go about my business and be myself. They asked me for autographs, and that was okay. That is not a problem. It was refreshing that the guys gave me a pass on that question.

On Friday I had the interview with the game announcers from Fox. They came into the office and talked to the team. They asked me about my future and talked a little about the past. We talked about the past, present, and future. It was a good production meeting. It was probably a little bit longer than usual, but it was good nonetheless.

Hines Ward was due to talk to them after me. He came in and tried to rush me out of there, trying to push me out. He was laughing at me for taking so long. I told him if he cried for me I wouldn't go. We badgered each other back and forth, but we love to kid around like that. It was pretty funny. It was an uneventful Friday. After practice I went to Blockbuster, and Trameka and I watched a movie in bed and got some pizza. We just had a date night at home. We watched *War of the Worlds*. It was a pretty good movie.

On Saturday things started to really heat up. Family and friends started to come in town. My mom and dad, my sister, my brother and his family, my aunt, my cousin and her husband from Atlanta, some friends of the family, and some of my friends all showed up. A good friend of mine, Deral Boykin, who was a teammate of mine with the Rams, flew in from Miami and surprised me. He said if it was the last home game he wanted to see the beginning and the end. That was neat. My high school buddy and business manager, Jahmal Dokes, drove in from Detroit with his wife. Another good friend, Odell Winn, flew in from Houston. A good group flew in from Houston. Lou Oppenheim came in from New York.

I knew it was going to be a busy Saturday, so I tried to get a nap in early. I was trying to coordinate everything from tickets to meals to lodging, and on top of everything else, it was New Year's Eve.

I left home early and headed to the hotel where we stay before the games. I got a chance to relax, so that was good. The New Year came in with me in the hotel room playing cards with a couple of teammates. I didn't really think about the game. I was just doing so many other things on Saturday that the thought of playing the last game didn't factor in. I got a good night's rest. I never have trouble sleeping.

Hines Ward and I are great friends. I loved his work ethic and dedication from the very start and would like to think I've been something of a mentor to him.

BETTIS ON HINES WARD

When Hines came in as a rookie, he was a hard worker, and that's what I gravitated toward. I liked his work ethic. He was a great guy to be around because he was totally committed. He started on special teams and worked his way up. He always has a great attitude about things. He is always smiling and upbeat, and I liked that about him. He wasn't doing what he wanted to be doing at the start, but he accepted his role and was willing to go out there and do it.

Our friendship started then and really developed from there. You hear so much about him being a hell of an athlete, but he is also a good person. He has always been conscious of everything that is going on around him, and that is important. We really hit it off well and really started to hang out outside of football.

We have become great friends. We do a lot together. Our families are friends, and I know we will be friends for a long time.

The last couple of years, knowing that he was becoming the face of the franchise in terms of being a leader, I wanted to walk him through some of the pitfalls and the successes that come with it. I thought that was important for me to do. It's fun to be a mentor in a way, to give him some help and show him what to expect along the way. I think he can take over the leadership role now. He understands what his job is and the importance of what he is doing. That's in good hands now.

THE DAY HAS ARRIVED

On Sunday I got up in the morning and I asked my father if he would make breakfast for me, something he used to do when I was little. I told him it beat the pregame meal that we get at the hotel. He said it was no problem. I went home, and Dad was cooking breakfast. We talked for a little while. Trameka came down with Jada, and I spent a little bit of time playing with Jada on the couch. We had breakfast, and after that I had the chance to sit on the couch and relax for a few minutes. I closed my eyes to think about everything. It's hard to reflect before a game. I didn't want to spend too much time doing it, but I wanted to take a second to look and understand that it could be the last game. I kicked my feet up for a minute. I was just thinking about my career and all of the years I played and the brief memories at Heinz Field since we left Three Rivers. I thought about the big games that we played and how this game was going to play out. I wanted to make sure we won because we had to go to the playoffs. I was thinking about everything that was taking place, everything that was important at that moment.

I then headed off to the game. When I was home, it was peaceful and restful spending time with the family, but once I got in the car it got hectic in a hurry. I was bombarded with phone calls about tickets, and I was on the phone for three-quarters of the drive working out all the logistics. I was running late as it was, and then I started getting call after call about tickets—who gets how many, where they'll be, and so on. I only had 20 tickets in my suite and another six outside, so it wasn't possible to satisfy all the requests I got, but I did the best I could.

I got to the stadium and the fans were outside near the parking lot. When I hit the stadium parking lot, though, my focus went right to the game. My mind didn't wander off at all. People were yelling and screaming, and I gave a wave. I then jumped into the shuttle that takes personnel to the entrance. On my way into the stadium I got a chance to talk to Matt Millen, the general manager of the Lions. He stopped me, and we had a nice conversation. He was talking about when it was time for him to walk away from the game and recalling memories of being at the Redskins and not being able to do a lot. He said a year later he thought about coming back. He told me, if you still want to play, then play. You can't turn back the clock. Once it's over, you get one opportunity and have to live and die with it. That was a good chat.

By the time I got to the locker room I was really late, so I was rushing. Before the game all of the running backs go out for a little workout. I was running around like a chicken with its head cut off getting ready. I got taped up and all ready and dashed out to the field with Verron Haynes and Willie Parker. As soon as I hit the field the crowd went crazy. It was like a rock concert as I was going around the field. People

Walking out of the tunnel for the Lions game was the most emotional part of the day for me. I knew I'd be on the field again someday, but this was probably my final trip out of the tunnel.

were getting up out of their seats and cheering me as I went around the stadium. That's when I had the chance to see a lot of the signs that were out there that the fans had made. It wasn't overly emotional yet because I was getting into game mode. I didn't expect that many signs. There were so many, and they were so thoughtful. I didn't get to read them as much as I wanted, though, because I was trying to warm up. I went back in then, got my pads on, and looked at my locker. I saw the Game Day program, and I was on the cover of it with a montage of pictures. It was pretty cool. I liked that. Verron had me sign a couple. I was messing with him for making me do it before the game.

When we went out on the field to stretch as a team everything slowed down. I had the chance to read some of the signs that were close to me. I had seen them earlier but hadn't had a chance to really read them. I got that feel-good feeling that you get from something like that.

Then it was back into the locker room to get ready for the game. When I walked into the locker room Coach Cowher came to me and told me they were going to announce me last with the starters, even though I didn't start. I thought that was a special and thoughtful gesture. I was moved by that and really appreciated it. He also told me they were going to do things on the JumboTron, but would only do it at times when the game was in the balance.

It was time for the introductions. Whenever I'd walk out, I'd always ask my fullback to walk with me, and I was thinking that might be the last time I'd walk out behind Dan Kreider. He guided me out, and when we got to the base of the stadium where we head out to the field, I had the chance to kind of take everything in. I was trying to get a snapshot of everything.

Just before the introductions, Joey Porter told me to call up all of the guys. I told them I just wanted to let everybody know that the most important thing about this game was that we needed to win. We had to get to the playoffs. I told the guys this opportunity is here, we have to seize it, that it is not promised to us. We have to win the football game. I led the team and we broke and were out of the huddle.

One by one guys were being introduced, and with every guy I started getting more and more psyched. My emotions were starting to get the best of me. I was trying to get a feel for the gravity of the moment. When I was the only one in the tunnel, I said a prayer and looked out at the stadium for what could be my last time, trying to get a mental picture that I could preserve forever in my mind. It was an awesome moment. They called my name, and I got goose bumps all over my body. It was an explosion of emotion, and I was off. I was going crazy. I could hear the crowd going crazy, too. I sped out there, sprinted down the field, knocked a cameraman over, and didn't even feel it. I went to the end zone and found my family up in their suite. I went to the sideline and Ben Roethlisberger told me that since I had already knocked one guy out, he thought I was ready to play.

When I was coming out of the tunnel the emotions were at an all-time high. That was the most emotional time of the whole day. I knew realistically that it would be the last time I would have the chance to come out of that tunnel. I knew there would be other times I would be out on the field and opportunities to be among the guys, but that would be the last time coming out of the tunnel. I'll never forget that moment. It's something I'll carry with me forever.

IT'S GAME TIME

The game started, and I was anxious to get an opportunity. Since we were playing Detroit, I knew the people back home would be watching. The first opportunity came when we got down to the red zone. They gave me the ball, and I scored the first touchdown. At that point I was thinking that this was a great way to end the day, with a touchdown. I was thinking this was a great ending to the story if this should be the end of the road. Then the opportunity came for me to score the second touchdown, and I thought, "Oh man, that was easy." They didn't put up much resistance. The crowd was really screaming now because I had scored two touchdowns.

My uncle from Detroit had called me the day before the game. He is a Lions fan and has always been a Lions fan. Whenever we played Detroit, he always hoped that the Lions would win but that I personally would have a good game. He said this was the first time he wanted us to win and for me to have a good game. After the second touchdown I thought about what my uncle had said and knew we had an opportunity to win this game.

Then I had the chance to score a third touchdown. It was the icing on the cake. It was incredible, but all the while I was having success, the crowd and fans were incredible in terms of the response I was getting. There were so many signs. I was trying to read some of them and enjoy the moment. It was so much. The crowd got more and more involved with every touchdown. After I scored my third touchdown it was an absolute frenzy. I looked up to my suite, and the majority of the men up there had their shirts off. I wondered what in the world was going on. They were going crazy. The people running the JumboTron were putting up stats and video highlights of me on the scoreboard, and the crowd was going nuts. The response of the fans was electric, and I was thrilled and gratified but also taken aback and humbled by it all.

Once the game actually started, it couldn't have gone much better for me. I had the good fortune of scoring three touchdowns, and the crowd was in an absolute frenzy. It was an emotional day and a fairy-tale ending for me at Heinz Field.

In the fourth quarter they gave a video tribute to my career. That was one of those times I appreciated it greatly, but I couldn't let it take me out of the game. I was done for the day, but we were still playing. I took a look at it, enjoyed it, but I still knew there was a lot of football left. It was one of those moments that was sweet, but it wasn't the ultimate, because by winning this game we had more football to play.

Those were moments I will never forget. The way the crowd responded as they were chanting "one more year"—for the whole crowd to get that loud, that was pretty special. I didn't even see the reaction from my teammates while it was going on. I was trying to bury myself and kind of disappear because I knew they wouldn't stop. I was in my own little world, but the cameraman stayed on me and kept showing me on the scoreboard.

I could never have imagined that kind of response and the type of respect that was given that day, especially from the number of jerseys and signs in the stands. What was fun was to look in the stands and not just see the No. 36 jerseys, but to see the old, ancient No. 36 jerseys with the square numbers from before we changed to what we wear now. You knew that was an old jersey they had to dust off and pull out of that bottom drawer of Steelers memorabilia. It was an oldie but a goodie. It made me feel good when I saw those jerseys because that meant people had kept them for a long time and they wanted to honor me. It was special.

Willie Parker even had my jersey on. He told me before the game that he was wearing it, but I didn't see it until after the game. It was an old Rams jersey he wore. It meant a lot that he did that. It was like him paying homage and saying, "This is what I think of you, wearing your old jersey on your day just to kind of represent you." That was fun to see.

After the game things were crazy. I didn't know what it was going to be like, but I had all kinds of players, my teammates included, wanting to get their picture taken with me. I didn't expect it or realize that it would happen. Teammates were coming over saying they needed a picture with me. The coaches were coming over to me expressing their feelings. It was a very emotional and significant time in the sequence of events that occur as a long career draws to a close. It was an opportunity for everyone to get that one keepsake picture, expecting that this might be one of their last opportunities. It was kind of weird because normally you don't have these people coming over saying, "Can I take a picture with you?" But it was great nonetheless. I was able to get pictures with people I wouldn't have thought to—some of the doctors, staff, and others. It was a unique opportunity.

GAME 16 VS. DETROIT, JANUARY 1, 2006

	1	2	3	4	Score
Detroit	14	0	7	0	21
Pittsburgh	14	7	14	0	35

Coming off the field after the game I looked at the field and took some snapshots of the scene. I tried to gather it all in. I wanted to have that image of going through the tunnel and up to the locker room. I wanted the mental memories.

When we got into the locker room I called the guys up and just told them not to worry about whether I would be there or not. I told them I would always be there with them, that I would always bleed black and gold. Some of us broke down. Joey Porter usually gathers everyone together, but he told me to do it. That was special.

I then went off to do my postgame press conference. It was a lot of what I expected, and I fielded a lot of questions. There was one moment, however, that really touched me. My father was brought into the interview room and sort of stood there in the middle of everything, and we made eye contact. It was one of those things my dad usually doesn't get to see. For him to be there was nice. He got a chance to see what I do off the football field. It was pretty significant.

After the press conference I went to see my family. It was calmer by then; everything was done. I decided to take them out on the field. For all of the years I had been playing, they had never been on the field. They always came to games but were never on the field. I wanted them to see what I see, from my level. They got to see the field; they looked up and saw the suite. They got to see the whole picture that I had seen for 13 years. I wanted to give them the opportunity to see it because, when it is all said and done, I will see the game now the way they have seen it for 13 years. I wanted to give them the chance to see it for just one moment the way I did for 13 years.

We took a lot of pictures down on the field. I got my picture with family and close friends. It was special. Everyone really enjoyed it.

As we were walking off the field, I was thinking, "This is it. I am one of the last ones out." It just felt appropriate for the moment. The crowds were gone. The sounds had disappeared. The praise was gone. It was just the stadium, the seats, the grass, and the moment. Just to be in that situation was special.

Then I heard some voices, but I couldn't figure out where they were coming from because there were only a few people still around. I looked up and saw two or three guys in the top row of the stadium starting to clean. As I was heading to the tunnel to leave, they started yelling, "One more year!" In a 60,000-seat stadium, to hear those lone voices yelling, "One more year!" was amazing.

Photo courtesy of AP/Wide World Photos.

I then headed out with the family to get home. I didn't want to start thinking about how it would feel when I went through all that again for my last game ever, whenever that might be. I just didn't want to think about what that would be like.

I stuck with my postgame ritual, which is to head home with the family after stopping at Wendy's on the way to get sandwiches. We do that after every game. I know it sounds crazy, but that's what I do. I'm a creature of habit. When I got home I turned my cell phone off. I just wanted to spend time with my family. I wanted to relax and not be bothered with outside stuff. When I did finally check my phone, my messages were full. There were a lot of messages congratulating me. I went through them all and listened to everything. It was great. There were a lot of nice messages.

REFLECTIONS IN THE
REARVIEW MIRROR

I feel so fortunate to have been among that elite group of young men who played football for the University of Notre Dame, and I will forever cherish every memory I have from my time in South Bend.

Photos courtesy of the Bettis family.

It's Time for Revenge

There wasn't much time for the team to celebrate our victory or dwell on our last game. We didn't have that luxury because we had to get ready to play the Bengals in the wild card playoff game. That was now the focus. I just wanted to focus on Cincinnati.

That Monday I did my radio show again. It was pretty crowded. The fans were doing a lot of yelling, and chanting, "One more year." It was wild. It was one of the largest crowds of the year. On Tuesday night I did my TV show, and it was the same thing. There were a lot of people there. It was extremely loud. They were there showing their support, showing how much they appreciated what I had done in my career.

On Wednesday, it was all about the Bengals. We definitely had something to prove. We wanted to prove that we were still the big dogs on the block. The one game that they won didn't signify anything. Once we found out they were the team we were going to play for the wild card, we were really looking forward to it. We were excited about it. When we figured out we were going to play Cincinnati, it was a fun day because we knew we wanted to get out there and go after those guys.

There was a lot of talk. We knew they felt that they were a better team. Bengal Carson Palmer made some comments after the first game we played them, which we won, and they still felt like they were the better team after we beat them. Then T.J. Housmenzadah, their wide receiver, used a Terrible Towel to wipe his shoes as he was leaving our stadium the last time we played. Based on a lot of the stuff they were saying after the second game, we knew that they really felt they were the dominant team, and we were determined to show them otherwise. They beat us that time because we had four turnovers, and that's what determined the outcome. The game was not decided by them flat out beating us.

The game started off in a tough way with Palmer being injured. My first reaction was disbelief. I then thought how thankful I was to be able to play this long and not have that kind of knee injury. I couldn't believe I was finishing 13 years and hadn't had a career-threatening injury. The way that I play and practice I was just thinking it's dangerous. It's a lot more dangerous than we let on. We think, "If it hasn't happened to me, then it's okay." But the possibility clearly exists. It brought a lot of thoughts to my mind.

We lost Quincy Morgan in the game, too. It was hard to see it happen. You want your teammates to be a part of things in the playoffs and experience everything the way that you will. When somebody goes down like that, a guy who has never been in the playoffs, you really wish it hadn't happened. You want him to enjoy the opportunity he was given.

The Bengals got out to an early lead, and we knew we were going to have to take their punch and that they would have the crowd behind them early. We knew we would have to settle in and play a smart football game. They went up 10–0, and we answered with a touchdown. They came back with a touchdown. We came back with another touchdown and kept the game close before halftime.

We went into the locker room feeling confident we had taken their best punch, and it was now time for us to punch back. We were chomping at the bit to get out of that locker room. There was no concern at all in there. It was just confidence. Guys knew we took their best shot, and we were only down by three. Now it was time to turn it on and show them what we are made of. That is what the thoughts were.

When the Bengals missed their field goal in the second half, you could see that the team was dejected and it was time for us to take advantage of that. Because of their inexperience in the playoffs, we knew that if we could get up on them it would probably be the end of them. Not having playoff experience gives you the thought you have to do too much. It put pressure on them, at home, being down. The goal was to get that turnover and get the ball into the end zone by any means necessary. We methodically marched down the field, converting some key third downs, and I was able to punch it in from the 5-yard line.

That drive really changed the momentum of the game. From there on, everyone in the stadium knew the Bengals were not coming back.

It felt good to score in a playoff game. You get extra satisfaction because you give your team a better chance at winning. Whenever you can score a touchdown in the playoffs it means a lot more. That makes you realize you are one step closer to realizing your dream of playing in and winning a championship.

Our next touchdown came on a pass to Cedrick Wilson. Antwaan Randle El got the ball on the snap and tossed it back to Ben Roethlisberger, who then threw it to Cedrick for a touchdown. At first I was thinking, "What

After the first two games between us and some of the things that were said and done, we were determined to prove to the Bengals that we were the better team, and we did.

The key to the game, I believe, was our third-quarter drive after their missed field goal. We marched down the field, and I was able to score from five yards out.

DRIVING HOME

are you doing?" Then I thought, "Great job!" I didn't know the play was called, and I didn't know what they were doing. It went from "What is going on?" to pure exhilaration. It was a big play.

That touchdown put the nail in the coffin. After that you could sense a difference. You could hear a pin drop in the stadium. It was dead silent. The fans knew the game was over. Fans were filing out of the stadium. That was the dagger.

I had a chance in the game to throw a touchdown pass, but it didn't work out for me. It was a halfback pass that was doomed from the snap. The snap was a little late, and the toss was a little behind me. I bobbled it really bad. By the time my eyes came up, I saw the fullback instead of Heath Miller. By the time I saw Heath, I realized I was about to get hit in the face, so I let the ball go and it hit the dirt. It was an all-around bad play, and I have to take the blame for that, but fortunately the game turned out okay. They showed the replay on the news a lot. I was so upset with myself for letting that happen.

Coming off the field after the game was emotional. We had gotten all kinds of criticism going into the game. I had always had a lot of success against the Bengals, and to have it again was tremendously gratifying. I kind of let out my emotions coming off the field, yelling and letting out the energy.

In the locker room afterward Coach Cowher yelled, "Who dey?" and we replied "We dey!" in reference to the cheer the Bengals do. It didn't surprise me he did that. In our meeting on Friday he indicated he was going to say something after the game if we won, but instead he let his frustration out like that.

REFLECTIONS IN THE REARVIEW MIRROR

There was a time when my family (I'm pictured here with my dad, mom, and brother John) tried to steer me toward a career in bowling rather than football—something about not wanting me to get hurt, they said. Fortunately, I was drafted by the Los Angeles Rams in the first round of the 1993 NFL draft, and I was able to prove it to be a pretty good career choice.

Top photo courtesy of Getty Images; bottom photo courtesy of the Bettis family.

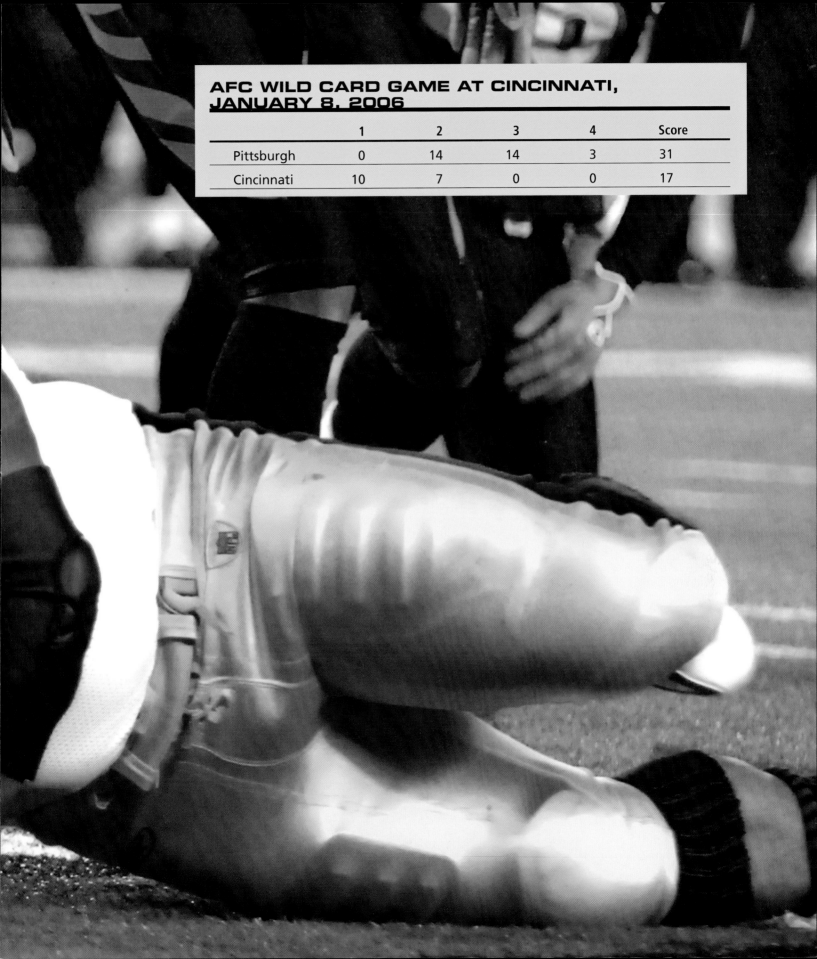

AFC WILD CARD GAME AT CINCINNATI, JANUARY 8, 2006

	1	2	3	4	Score
Pittsburgh	0	14	14	3	31
Cincinnati	10	7	0	0	17

A Chance at Redemption

Going into the division playoffs

against the Colts we were very much aware that the last time we played them we didn't play a complete game. We were very disappointed in the way we had played and just grateful that we were given another shot at them. We knew we were a better team than we showed in the previous game, and we were licking our chops at the opportunity to get back in there and prove it. We knew we were going to play better.

It didn't matter to us that we were the underdog. We didn't use that in terms of motivation. The motivation was that they were the best team in the NFL and that they beat us up the last time, and we were not going to let it happen again. That was our motivation.

The week leading up to the game there was an action shot of me on the cover of *Sports Illustrated*. In all my years of playing I was on the cover only one time before, and that one was staged at a photo shoot. It was never an action shot. To see it was like, wow. Then the questions came about the jinx—people say that players featured on the cover play badly or lose their next time out. I didn't pay that any mind though. I was honored *Sports Illustrated* wanted me on the cover.

In practice that week we knew we were going to be able to take advantage of some of the things the Colts do defensively, but we never knew we would come out on offense like we did in that game. When it happened, it was great, but that wasn't really the plan.

The feeling when we left the locker room before the game was pretty unique. There was a calm confidence. Guys were warming up, not saying much. There was a feeling we were getting ready to do something special. I could feel it. I really noticed it.

When the game started and we jumped on them fast, you could tell it was because of that focus. I knew when we jumped out we were going to be in good shape. But it wasn't over early. I knew it was going to be a long game. We knew they had an explosive offense and they could score

I was able to score a touchdown in the third quarter of the playoff game against the Colts, but then my rare fumble late in the game nearly helped them send the game into overtime.

quickly. There wasn't a sense that we had the game in the bag, but we were glad to have breathing room.

In the first game against them our defense played well, but our offense didn't give them any help. That was part of the problem. We didn't give them any help. In this game our offense kept Peyton Manning off the field. Joey Porter had made some comments earlier in the week that the Colts were soft, so our defense went out there to prove Porter was right. We knew the defense was going to take it to them, and we had to hold up our end of the deal.

In the second half the Colts started to come back. We knew eventually they were going to score, but the key was for us to keep it going offensively. We had to make sure we kept putting points on the board.

With less than a couple of minutes left in the game, the Colts had the ball backed up inside their own 10-yard line. The defense had been swarming Manning all afternoon, and they ended up sacking him on fourth down at the Colts' 2-yard line, where we got the ball back. We had the ball first-and-goal at their 2-yard line, and all we had to do was score to ice the game. All I could think about was protect the ball, score a touchdown, and the game is over. We got in the huddle, and the coaches called the counter play, a play we've run a thousand times, so I was pretty confident. The play was designed for me to go behind Alan Faneca. Alan turned up early, and I kept going. By the time I got to the hole, Colt Gary Brackett was there. He was so low I knew I couldn't run him over, so I tried to go inside of him. By the time I turned my body sideways he went to tackle me and his helmet hit the ball clean, right on my hand, and it popped the ball out. All I could see was the ball going up in the air as I was going backward. I was thinking to myself, "This can't be happening. I cannot believe this. This is exactly what we couldn't do." Nick Harper picked up the football for the Colts and started heading the other way with it. All I was thinking was, "Please, someone, please tackle this guy. Get him down and give our defense a chance." I looked up and I saw the guy getting tackled, and I realized Ben Roethlisberger made the tackle.

I was so dejected after that fumble, I didn't know what to do. It could easily have been the last play of my career. I was thinking, "If my career ends like this, I don't know if I'll ever be able to live it down."

As I headed to the sideline, I kept thinking, "Oh my God, I fumbled the football." I just couldn't believe it. I couldn't believe I fumbled the football. I must have said it a thousand times: I can't believe I fumbled the football. It was like I was in the twilight zone. I was down on one knee, the defense was out there, and I knew the cameras would be watching and I had to keep my head up. If this was to be the last play of my career, then

Mike Vanderjagt's missed field goal at the end of regulation enabled us to hold on for the win—and got me off the hook! *Photo courtesy of AP/Wide World Photos.*

AFC DIVISIONAL PLAYOFF AT INDIANAPOLIS, JANUARY 15, 2006

	1	2	3	4	Score
Pittsburgh	14	0	7	0	21
Indianapolis	0	3	0	15	18

I guess it was meant to be, but I sure wasn't too happy about it. That's how I made peace with myself. Guys came up to me and said things, but I was in a daze and didn't pay attention to what anybody said.

The Colts got the ball, and I sat there watching, still stunned and in disbelief, filled with so much anxiety. But thankfully the defense held them and it was fourth down. I knew then at best they could only tie the game, so I started thinking it was time for me to get myself together. If we got the ball back we were going to have to score to win. When fourth down came I did feel better. It gave us another opportunity.

Before the kick Antwaan Randle El came over and told me the Colts' kicker, Mike Vanderjagt, was going to miss the field goal. It was a 46-yarder, and usually Vanderjagt, one of the best kickers in the league, would make the kick, but sure enough, it went wide right. I started jumping up and down with the rest of the guys, yelling, "He missed it! He missed it! I can't believe he missed it!" I knew then that the fumble wasn't going to be the last word. My hands went up in the air, and I kept thinking that since I was running off the field, the game must indeed be over.

After the game, guys came over and hugged me. Coach Cowher hugged me and told me I'd be carrying the ball again, and that they were going to get me to Detroit, where the Super Bowl was to be played.

My career could have ended on that one play, one play where I went out on the field confident, even arrogant, that I'd get the ball and score the game-cinching touchdown. Instead, I turned the football over at the worst possible time and almost cost my team the game. I learned a valuable lesson: if you go out there with a sense of arrogance and accomplishment before you've accomplished anything, then you set yourself up for failure.

I found out a few days after the game that a guy had a heart attack after I fumbled. It wasn't because he was upset about the game: it was because he thought it might be the last play of my career. It made me realize how much people follow everything you do and how much people appreciate you. Sometimes it is hard to see that. But for people to be concerned that that could have been my last play and not wanting to see my career end that way, that was touching. It tells you people care about you as a person, not just a football player. It struck me to the core. Later I was fortunate enough to be able to talk to him and find out what a die-hard fan really is like. I was very thankful for that opportunity.

Because of the significance of the play and how it happened, I knew people would talk about it a lot. Every single day leading up to the Denver game I was asked about it. I knew I wouldn't be able to stop talking about it until the first snap of the next game. Everybody

A man's allowed to dance a little bit after scoring a touchdown in the AFC Championship game, which I did in the second quarter. *Photo courtesy of AP/Wide World Photos.*

Speaking of Denver, we were back now where we were a year ago, playing in the AFC Championship game. We had to make it count this time. It wasn't so much being happy about going to the AFC Championship game as it was a step toward our number-one goal. Having lost a couple of them before I think it made us concentrate that much more. We had to win the game. We had to get to the Super Bowl.

I think everybody felt the disappointment the year before. It was very clear, and it wasn't something to forget easily. The feeling was fresh, and I think it gave us an edge going into the game.

The night before the game I talked to the team. I told them there were two things I wanted to tell them. The first was that all each of us had to do was just give 110 percent. If after the game you can say you gave 110 percent, I am going to shake your hand, give you a big hug, and tell you thank you. Don't take anything with you. Leave it all out on the field. Don't leave the field with anything left. That's all I could ask. Winning that game wasn't going to take a special effort from anybody on the team. It was just going to take everybody being consistent and doing what they had been doing all year. If everyone did his job, there was no way we were going to lose that football game. I told them some people say success is when preparation meets opportunity, but that's not true. Preparation doesn't meet opportunity; you have to seize the opportunity and take it.

The last thing I told them was to take me home to Detroit. I told them to please take me home. And I also promised dinner at my mom's house on me.

I think they all responded to my speech, and we went out and won the AFC Championship.

There was a lot of talk about us being the road team for the third time in a row for this game. Many people thought it might take the pressure off of us. I didn't necessarily agree with that. I think what it did was

Back at It Again

interviewed me about it. It was the last thing I wanted to be thinking about going into the AFC Championship game, but I understood. It's the price you pay when you make a mistake.

The media were showing the fumble on television every day. They showed it up until the morning of the Denver game. I was in the hotel the morning of the game and they were going to show it yet again, but I turned off the TV. I didn't need to see it again.

REFLECTIONS IN THE REARVIEW MIRROR

I had two straight 1,000-yard rushing seasons with the Rams in my first two years in the NFL, and then I moved to the Steelers after the 1995 season. Pittsburgh fans, both young and old, really embraced the Bus right from the start. *Top photo courtesy of Getty Images; bottom photo courtesy of the Bettis family.*

AFC CHAMPIONSHIP GAME AT DENVER, JANUARY 22, 2006

	1	2	3	4	Score
Pittsburgh	3	21	0	10	34
Denver	0	3	7	7	17

give us a better focus. Our football team was better focused and tougher mentally this time compared to last. I think that is why we were able to go on the road and have the success we had.

Getting out on the field on game day was kind of surreal. Having been there before, it wasn't as big, but it was more of a game. That was a big benefit of playing in it the year before. I think the year before it was a bigger deal in terms of the hoopla. This year the game was nothing out of the ordinary for us. You can't say experience isn't a factor. It does make a difference. That game compared to the year before was totally different in our mind-set and how we approached it.

This game was tough for me because of my asthma and the altitude in Denver. They didn't call their old stadium Mile High Stadium for nothing. I did treatments every day leading up to the game, when normally I would take the treatment only on game day or at halftime. In Denver I needed it every day because of the thinness of the air. Even with treatment, it was still difficult to breath there. I was always struggling to catch my breath. Having played there before, I knew it would be tough.

After the game got started it spiraled out of control for Denver. They turned the football over a couple of times in the first half. Our offense was determined to put points on the board. We were so ready, so well coached, and so prepared for that game that we came out and everything they did we had an answer for. We were rolling. We executed our game plan, and the defense played excellently. It was domination from start to finish. For the most part the game was determined at halftime. Our guys were so focused and ready to play, it showed.

When the game was ending, I couldn't believe it. I was saying to myself, "We are going to the Super Bowl; I am going home." My thoughts were on my family, which was always there. I looked up at them and said, "We're going home." It was a great feeling. We were going to the Super Bowl. For a lot of years we had some great football teams here, and we always fell short by just a little bit. For us to finally reach the goal was incredible. I was giddy like a kid on the sideline. Duce Staley and I got a chance to give Coach Cowher the ceremonial shower. That was fun.

The first half of the mission was accomplished—getting to the Super Bowl. The second half would be winning the game.

The flight back from Denver was a riot. Everybody was so upbeat. Every five minutes someone was yelling out, "We are going to the Super Bowl!" It seemed like we landed only minutes after taking off from Denver. That's how quick the flight went.

DETAILS, DETAILS, DETAILS

We came in on Monday morning and got all of our Super Bowl information. Needless to say, we were pretty excited about it. We couldn't help but have fun with it all: where we were staying, the practice schedule, the routine—it was all a joy because we were going to the Super Bowl. It was what we had been playing for, what we had sacrificed and sweated for since training camp in July.

Everyone gets a set number of tickets. It was tough for me to see how many tickets we were allocated, but I couldn't complain. I would never complain. I was asked for tons of tickets. I must have had at least a hundred requests. But if the ticket requests were the worst part, I am a lucky man. I couldn't take care of everybody, but I established a priority system and did what I could.

The list of media requests for the week before we left for Detroit was long. Everybody wanted to do a sit-down interview; everybody wanted to talk; everybody had questions. But you can only do so much. I did as much as I could do. I figured that was the time to do it so that when it was time to focus on the game, I could.

I had a few commercials to shoot, too. I did an NFL commercial, a mortgage company commercial, a Disney commercial, and a commercial for the American Lung Association and GlaxoSmithKline.

The Disney commercial was fun. It was in preparation for a bunch of different players possibly becoming the MVP. They made us all practice that famous line, "I'm going to Disney World."

I think my parents had as many requests as I did. ESPN's *Cold Pizza* flew my parents from Denver to New York, and they were on the show the next day. I never even knew it until people told me about it later. They were the stars. Everybody was enamored with the fact that they had been to all of my games. The neat irony is that they didn't have to go anywhere for the Super Bowl.

When Thursday rolled around we got back to practice. That is what we were craving. We wanted to be out on the field. That was the good part. It got things back to normal. We were out there working our butts off and getting ready for the game.

Our fans are the best in sports; I truly believe that. And this guy obviously had it right in Denver that day. *Photo courtesy of AP/Wide World Photos.*

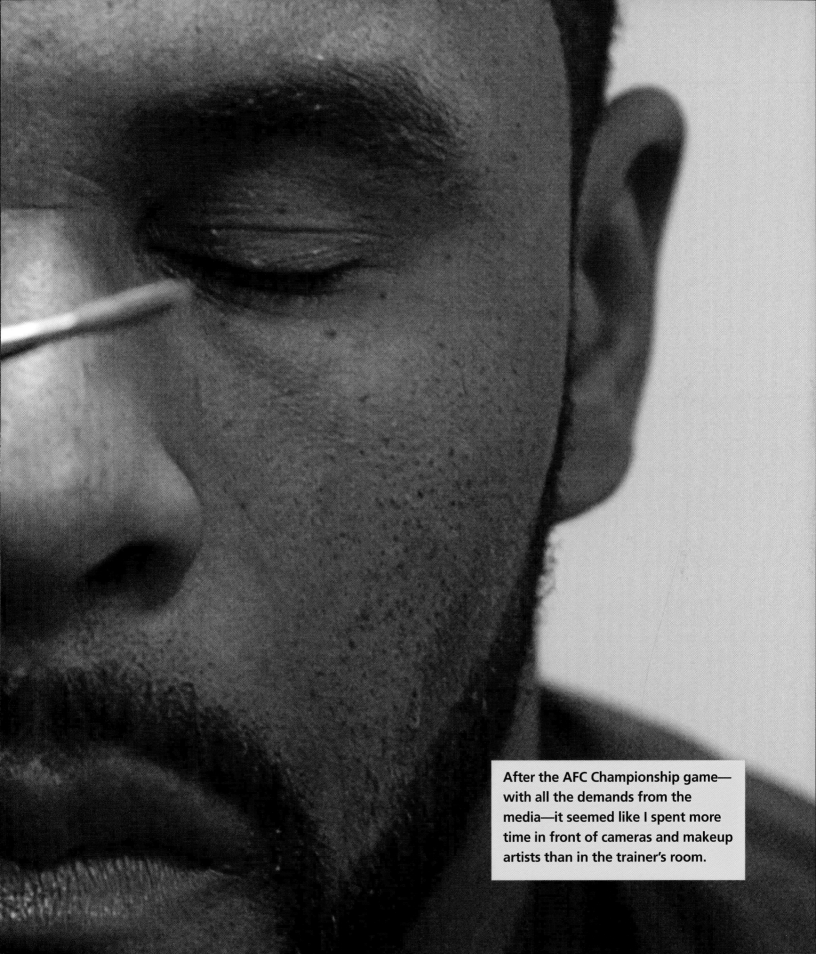

After the AFC Championship game—with all the demands from the media—it seemed like I spent more time in front of cameras and makeup artists than in the trainer's room.

On Saturday before we left we had the chance to buy some Super Bowl merchandise for our friends and families. I bought some Terrible Towels and lanyards for everyone to put their tickets in. I figured I didn't have to buy too much because it's in my hometown and they could buy everything there.

IT'S TIME TO SAY THIS IS IT

At some point around the 13th or 14th week of the season, Steelers chairman Dan Rooney had seen me heading out the front door of the practice facility and asked me to come up to his office sometime soon to talk to him. I told him I would, but I wasn't looking forward to it. I didn't really know what he wanted to talk about, but I knew what I'd have to tell him, and I wanted to put it off as long as possible. So I waited and procrastinated and made up one excuse after another. I just didn't want to have that conversation. As crazy as it seems, knowing it was going to be my last year—win, lose, or draw—I wanted to avoid the finality of it all. I am a football player, and no football player wants to walk away from the game.

A week went by, and then another week. Every time I saw Rooney I told him I would be in. The playoffs started, and I thought, "I should talk to him now," but I still delayed. I waited it out through the playoffs, and when it was time for the AFC Championship game I thought I couldn't put it off any longer, but somehow I found a way.

As the week was coming to a close and it was almost time for us to go to Detroit, I finally decided it was the right time. I didn't tell anyone I was doing it, not even Trameka. I went in and talked to Rooney. I wanted to thank him for being such a people person. There were a lot of times the organization could have chosen to go in a different direction, but they decided not to. Sometimes front-office people and owners can get caught up in numbers and stats and lose sight of the person. They never did that with me. I just wanted to tell him thank you for that and how much I appreciated everything he had done for me. It meant a lot to me. I let him know this was going to be it. He thanked me for everything that I had done and added that we weren't finished yet.

I went in and talked to Steelers president Art Rooney after that, and we had basically the same conversation. I wanted to explain to him that I appreciated them being there for me, coming to my aid, and caring about my well-being as a person. I let him know how much that meant to me.

I walked out of both meetings close to tears. The terrible finality of it all really hit me. I knew that the Super Bowl was going to be my last game. Those conversations with the Rooneys were very important to me, and I'm glad I had them.

My feelings going into the Super Bowl were bittersweet, especially when I finally had to tell Dan (pictured at right) and Art Rooney II (above) of my plans to retire. *Photos courtesy of AP/Wide World Photos.*

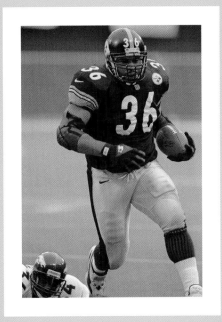

REFLECTIONS IN THE REARVIEW MIRROR

Probably my best season was in 1997, when I rushed for 1,665 yards and averaged 111 yards per game. Pictured below is my 45-foot custom tour bus from my foundation, The Bus Stops Here. This bus traveled to all the away games and brought smiles to all the kids who were able to ride it to the games. *Top photo courtesy of AP/Wide World Photos; bottom photo courtesy of the Bettis family.*

12

I'm Headed Home

We left for Detroit on Monday morning of Super Bowl week. I headed out to the airport, and as soon as I got to the security checkpoint I looked around and saw somebody wearing a green No. 6 jersey. It surprised me a bit, but not as much as when we got through security and I saw Joey Porter start pulling jerseys out of a huge garbage bag to pass out to all the guys. I asked him what he was doing, and he said it was only fitting that since we were going to my hometown everybody should wear my Notre Dame jersey. I was like, wow. I couldn't believe it. I didn't get the true extent of it until I got on the plane and I saw how many jerseys there actually were. I had only seen him pass out two or three of them and thought that was it. When I got on the plane there were dozens. I was taken aback by how much they thought of me to give me that kind of tribute. That was a special feeling, knowing that they wanted to do that for me.

We got to Detroit and it was really cool. When we landed I felt exhilarated—not only did we have the opportunity to play in the Super Bowl, but as we were getting off the plane all of these guys had my jersey on. It was incredible. There was so much anticipation. We got to the airport hangar and there was nothing but smiles. One, I was back home. But two, and most important, we were playing in the Super Bowl. I was like a seven-year-old kid getting off the plane and looking forward to what the week had in store for me.

When I touched down in Detroit my cell phone went black. I cut it off for the duration of the week, which was good. I didn't need the distraction. I had another cell phone for emergencies only, which made it much more manageable.

We headed from the airport out to Pontiac, Michigan, where we were staying. When we got to the hotel more media and quite a few fans were there. It was great to see it all. We got checked in, but there wasn't much time to rest. We went to the Silverdome, which was to be our practice facility, for a quick walk-through, just to get used to the place and become acquainted with it. When we got back we were still on the move because about six or seven of us had to head out to a press conference that was held at the media center in downtown Detroit. A lot of media were there waiting for us. I knew the media were going to be intense just because of the story line. I was prepared for it. I knew there would be a lot of questions. I wasn't too surprised by all of the reporters, the cameramen, and the photographers. This is what I had been hoping for all through my 13-year career. I just wanted to soak it all up. Had it been my first or second year, it might have been more overwhelming, but I was looking forward to everything that came with going to the Super Bowl.

Tuesday was media day. It was the first time for us to head to Ford Field where the game was to be played. We got there, and they took us right to the locker room. Going in there and seeing our jerseys hanging there with the Super Bowl XL patch made us feel like we had arrived. That was a great moment.

Before we went out to the interviews, some of us went around to do special things for the game broadcast. We had the chance to take some black-and-white still photos holding the Super Bowl trophy. It was an awesome experience. It was the first time I had held the Lombardi Trophy. I touched it and held it in a way that preserved the reverence that comes with the trophy. I was very careful with it, because I wanted to show the awesome amount of respect that I have for it. I knew that it wasn't mine, but more important, I understood what it stood for, what it meant. Just to be in the presence of the trophy was pretty awesome. I will never forget that experience.

After that we headed out to the field to talk to the media. There were about three thousand media people gathered there. It was crazy, but it was something I had looked forward to my entire football career. Every year I watched guys go through media day. I would always turn on the television on media day and watch guys like Warren Sapp, Ray Lewis, Terrell Davis, and Eddie George. There were many times when I thought it should have been me out there, and I would get somewhat resentful wishing it was. When it finally was my turn, I wanted every question to be asked. I wanted to be out there my full hour's worth with the media. I wanted people to keep asking me questions. I wanted to feel the same way those guys had felt in the past; I wanted to get all of the questions they got. It was a very spirited give-and-take. I wanted to have fun with it, and I did. It was great.

After the interviews ended we headed out onto the field for the team picture. It was hard because Duce Staley wasn't there for that. His father had died just days before, and he stayed home for the funeral and was due to arrive later in the week. It was tough getting the team picture

I was overcome with emotion when Joey Porter pulled out the No. 6 Notre Dame jerseys as we got off the plane in Detroit. That's Ben and me, arriving at the biggest game of our lives, and in ND style. *Photo courtesy of AP/Wide World Photos.*

The team photo before the Super Bowl, and my only regret is that Duce Staley wasn't able to be there.

There were so many commitments before the actual game that it wasn't even funny. But this soup commercial at least afforded me the opportunity to get some fun camera time with my mom and my good friend Donovan McNabb.

taken without him there. But what they did was get an intern to wear his uniform and just Photoshopped him into the picture later. It was good that they were able to find a way to get him in the picture, but still it would have been nice for Duce to be there. He was a guy who had been through so much to get to the Super Bowl. It was disappointing he couldn't be a part of it because of what he had to go through. He, more than anybody on this team, needed to go to the Super Bowl after playing in five championship games in a row and winning only this last one. He played in three NFC Championship games with the Eagles and lost and two with us, losing one and winning one. He deserved to be there and to be able to enjoy everything. It was important that he be a part of the team photo.

For me, the media blitz wasn't the end of my day. I had decided to get as much out of the way as possible on Tuesday. I wanted to take care of all of the obligations before we started practice on Wednesday, so Tuesday was the day for getting everything done. I had a commitment to do something for Campbell's Soup with my parents. My mom was in a commercial they did a few years ago, and they wanted my mother and me to do something that we had agreed to do long before we knew we were going to the Super Bowl. It was a fun deal with Donovan McNabb and his mother. We had a competition, and we won.

From there it was off to do an opening piece for ABC with Tom Jackson. We were walking around downtown doing it. I had to be wearing a suit for the piece, and I didn't have anywhere to change because we were staying in Pontiac. I found Ron Cook, a writer for the *Pittsburgh Post-Gazette*, and he let me change in his hotel room. I also caught a 15-minute catnap while I was there. I did the ABC piece and then rushed over from there to get the key to the city of Detroit, which was presented to me by the mayor. With all of the support I was getting from my home base of Detroit, this was really important to me. It meant a lot to get the key. It's where I am from and it's my city. To get a key to my own city was a real highlight.

Next I had to do an interview with HBO that was held in Dearborn at the Henry Ford Museum, which was a bit of a ride. The piece started with me on the bus that Rosa Parks actually rode when she was told she had to move to the back and refused. That was incredible. To be on that actual bus that started such a movement was so significant. Just to have the opportunity to walk through that bus was amazing.

After that we went all the way back downtown to do my normal television show, *The Jerome Bettis Show*. This was my last obligation of the day. We had a great turnout for the show. It was at Hockeytown, which is a downtown sports bar, and it was packed with Steelers fans. Frenchy Fuqua was a guest on the show, as were my parents.

I got to see a Pistons game while I was back home.

From the time I left the hotel at about 8:00 in the morning until about 9:00 at night, I had been on the go. I had my family there with me, which was great, but it was a draining day. I was in bed early Tuesday night and slept really well.

Wednesday it was more interviews, but these were held at the hotel in a tent set up outside. It wasn't so bad because it was so close. After that we left for the Silverdome for practice. It was good to get out on the field and be reminded of what we were really there for. It was a great start of the workweek for us. It was a good practice, and everyone was really feeling good about being out there.

Before the AFC Championship I told the guys if they got me to Detroit, dinner would be on me. So on Wednesday night my mom, with some help, made dinner for the guys at my parents' house. We took a few cars and a busload of guys over there. A ton of guys came. It was special that my mom got the opportunity to do her motherly duties that she likes to do. I enjoyed the food, but my real joy came from watching everybody else eat and watching my mother do her thing and enjoy it.

I videotaped a lot of the dinner, plus a lot of other things that week, just to capture the moment. I wanted something to remember it all by.

After dinner we went to the Pistons game. Walking into the Palace of Auburn Hills was a real rush, as was being acknowledged by the crowd and the organization. I already had a relationship with the Pistons, having gone to some games in the past, but they really were good to us. They gave us the best seats in the house, courtside at midcourt, and Pistons jerseys to wear. The ovation that we got when we came in was amazing. They kind of stopped the game as we went to our seats. You wouldn't think that football players would have that kind of impact at a basketball game. But the people all recognized us, and it was pretty awesome.

Thursday was the same schedule as Wednesday with regard to media interviews and practice. I got a little break during the interviews and went around with my video camera and tried to capture some of it. I interviewed some guys, even my running backs coach Dick Hoak.

I hosted a bowling tournament on Thursday night for The Bus Stops Here Foundation. As soon as I knew the Super Bowl was going to be in

Detroit, I knew I wanted to capitalize on the fact that there would be a lot of players in town. I was planning to put on the event no matter who was in the Super Bowl to raise money for my foundation, which works to help underprivileged children. Thursday was the perfect day, because if I didn't wind up in the Super Bowl, players that were in the game could still come, plus other players would have started to come to town by then. The event went great. It was a lot of fun. A lot of my teammates were able to come to it, some of them bowling and some just there to give their support.

Friday we didn't have any morning interviews, just went straight to practice. When we got back to the hotel ABC was set up there and we did the production meetings with the announcers and so forth. That was quick and easy and ended our commitments for that day. For a lot of the players, that was the day the families arrived in Detroit. Obviously mine was already there, so things were more settled for me.

Saturday was the final day of practice for us. We had our normal morning walk-through, and then the rest of the day we were on our own. Later in the afternoon we left the team hotel and headed to another hotel where it was just the team, minus all of the families and everyone else. It helped with the normalcy of what we always do on a road trip. We went into game mode once we got on the bus and went to the other hotel. It was all about football. At the first hotel there were so many other things going on. But when we got to the second hotel, we knew it was all about football, and the focus was on nothing but the task at hand.

Saturday night there was a strange mood. It was confident, but quiet. It was loose, guys were laughing, but it was quiet. In the team meeting you always hear some chirping. But this time there was dead silence. There was joking on the way in, but once we got in there a hush came over the room. Coach Cowher talked. He didn't give the rah-rah speech; he just told us what we needed to know. He told us nobody had to play special, just do what you do. He told us if we concentrated on being focused on our jobs, we would win. It was reconfirming what we already knew, that if we played our game they couldn't beat us. That's how the meeting went.

After that I went to my room to watch some television. NFL Network kept showing Super Bowl highlights. I watched a lot of them, including the one of Buffalo against Dallas. I actually was at that game. I was coming out of college and declared for the draft early, and I was at the Rose Bowl in Los Angeles in the stands watching that game. Watching them play on TV brought back some memories. As I was watching the highlights I had to pinch myself as a reminder that the next day I'd be playing in the same game. I was watching for certain things to really pay attention to. I went to sleep and slept like a baby. I slept like a log. I had an absolutely great night of sleep.

REFLECTIONS IN THE REARVIEW MIRROR

As Super Bowl XL neared, much ado was made about my roots in Detroit. These are present-day photos of my old high school (top) and my old grade school (bottom), which has since become a high school and plays its football games on Jerome Bettis Field. *Photos courtesy of AP/Wide World Photos.*

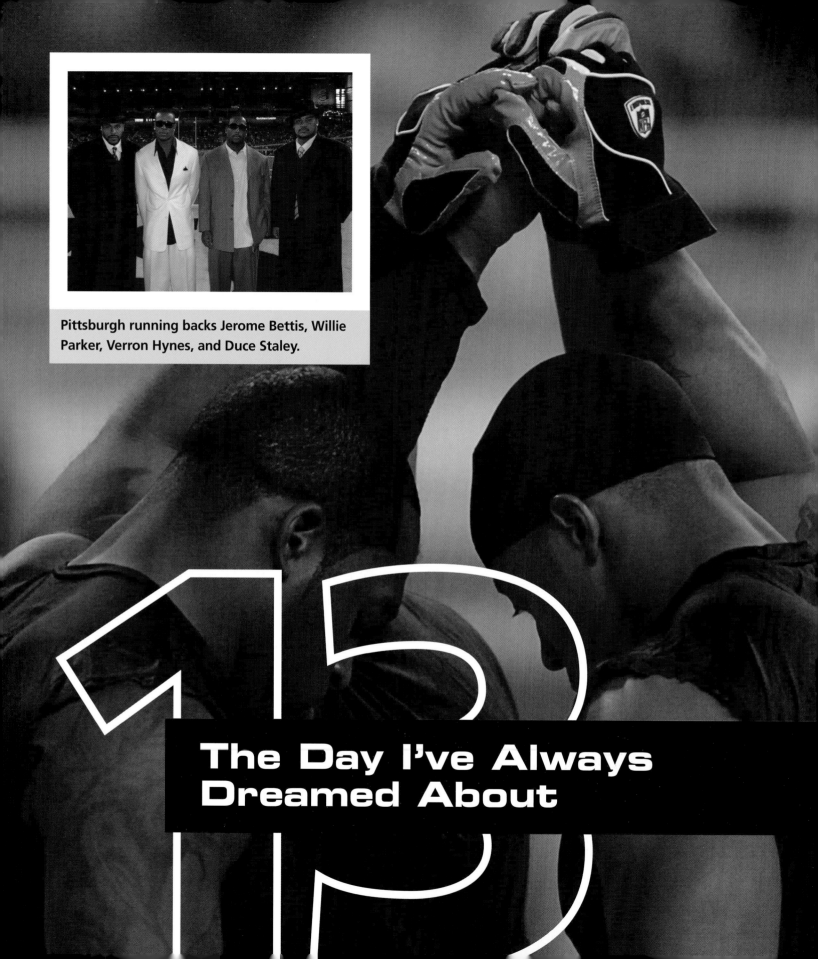

Pittsburgh running backs Jerome Bettis, Willie Parker, Verron Hynes, and Duce Staley.

The Day I've Always Dreamed About

My routine on game day wasn't unlike what it would have been for any other away game. My mom and dad came to the hotel just like they normally do to see me off. I got on the bus and just started talking up a storm with the guys.

When we got to the stadium the anticipation really started to build, and everything kicked into high gear once we got into the locker room. We saw the Super Bowl XL logo on everything—the helmets, the jerseys—all over the locker room. It was like, okay, this is it. We went out to warm up, and it was a sea of black and gold out there. I couldn't believe all of the fans in their Steelers stuff. I started doing my normal laps around the field like I do every game. I went a little slower this time and looked into the crowd a little bit more. As we went through warm-ups I felt more confident about the day. The running backs finished their warm-ups, and we went back into the locker room. I went into the training room to get taped, and it really started to hit me that we were playing in the Super Bowl. I was sitting on the training table thinking, "This is it."

It was the time I had been waiting for my entire career. We were ready to go out onto the field for intros. Just as we were heading out Joey Porter stopped everybody at the door and said, "Bus, I am going to hold everybody back, and you are going to go out there first and bring us in." He looked at me and said, "Give us everything you got." I was stunned. When I went out it was surreal. It was a longer run than normal because of all of the MVP banners, so I had to run a pretty good distance. I was screaming and going crazy and have never been so jacked up in my life. I turned around, thinking the guys were right behind me, but they were some ways back, and I thought, "Great, what do I do now?" I didn't know what was going to happen until we were introduced. I tried to take in as much as I could, but when I came out I was so emotional I didn't see everything. But I did see that crowd, and I saw how electric they were. The Terrible Towels were everywhere. I was so surprised how many fans we had there. I could have never envisioned that moment. I didn't know if we would ever get to the Super Bowl, much less a Super Bowl in my own hometown.

"This is it," I kept thinking...my last professional football game...the Super Bowl!

THE DAY I'VE ALWAYS DREAMED ABOUT

We started the game off slowly…

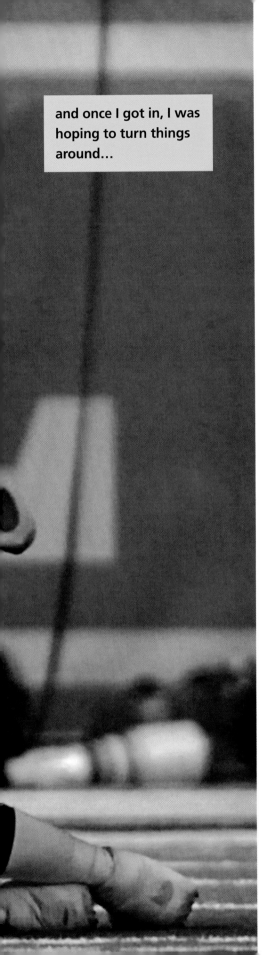

and once I got in, I was hoping to turn things around…

The game started off slow for us. I could tell we were a little bit tight, especially Ben Roethlisberger. Guys were dropping the ball, and we just weren't as sharp as we normally were. I was thinking that was exactly what Seattle needed for them to win, for us to come out and be flat. I knew we had to pick it up. If we were going to win the Super Bowl, we needed to be sharp. I knew we were struggling, that we weren't playing our best game. But when we went into halftime up 7–3, I felt like we had a good chance to win the game. We had played the worst half we probably could play, and we were still up. Normally we would be down playing like that. At that point I knew it was just a matter of us going in and refocusing, and that's exactly what we did.

We were anxious at halftime because we knew we were getting the ball back. We knew we had to get a drive going to get ourselves in position and try to take advantage of that. It took so long for halftime to finish. Usually halftime is really quick, but at the Super Bowl it's a lot longer. Guys had to reheat themselves because they had cooled down. It was strange. Coach had talked to us about how long it would be, but it still dragged on.

We had underachieved in the first half as a group. We weren't able to run the ball. We were dropping passes. I knew it was a matter of time for us. I didn't think we had to harp on it. Then the second half came and things started to turn around. It was a roller coaster of emotions. We went from being up to needing to stop the other team from scoring to win the game. We would get a drive going and then turn the ball over. Next thing we knew we created a turnover, and that was when everything started to pick up for us.

The key to us sealing the win was the touchdown pass from Antwaan Randle El to Hines Ward. When that play was called I was standing next to Coach Mark Whipple. He called it in, and I was dubious. I didn't think it was the right play at that point, but I sure was glad to be proved wrong. The play worked, and I changed my mind in a hurry and thought, "Great call." I had been thinking this was our chance to take some time off the clock, but boy was I wrong. There was a lot of excitement on the sideline then. We all were getting the feeling that we were going to win the game. I was thinking of all the years of hard work and sacrifice, and it finally was happening for us.

At the end of the game the Seahawks were trying to score, but the defense really held them. We knew this was it. There was so much joy in my heart then, unlike anything I had ever felt before. We had done something we set out to do at the beginning of the year. It was something I believed would happen. It was 13 years' worth of dreams coming true all in one moment. That moment in time was amazing. It was so special. That moment when the clock was ticking down and the

THE DAY I'VE ALWAYS DREAMED ABOUT

…and in the second half we were able to get rolling.

realization that we were Super Bowl champs was settling in, I had goose bumps all over me.

When the game ended the first guy I went over to was Hines, and we did a Disney World piece together. That was fun. I was living a dream, and that's where dreams come true. It was great for me. Disney had said that they were pretty sure if the Steelers won, then regardless of who the MVP was, they would probably take me as well and they would let me know after the game. After the game was over they told me I was going to Disney World with Hines.

After that we went for the trophy presentation. Man, when I got that trophy in my hands it symbolized that the journey was complete. When I held it, it was like all of the years of struggling, suffering, and pain had washed away. That was something. To hold that trophy in the air, it's something you dream about. As a kid you dream about it. Playing in the NFL you dream about it. You dream about holding the Lombardi Trophy.

Also, after the game I decided it was the perfect time to announce that my career was coming to a close. I did it right there on the podium in front of the fans, my teammates, everyone. I told them that it feels incredible. It's been an incredible ride. There always comes a time when you have to call it quits. I said the Bus's last stop is right here in Detroit. It all came right from the heart. I didn't know what I was going to say, and I didn't prepare anything in advance, but I knew that win or lose I would be saying something after the game.

I had to do a press conference right after the game. I think the media thought the moment swept me away when I was on the podium and that I said something that I really didn't want to say. But I meant it, and I told them again that this was it for me, that the Bus had made his last stop. The postgame press conference was the culmination of all of the media attention during the week. I was asked all kinds of questions. I didn't mind it at all. I enjoyed it. As weird as it sounds, I was looking forward to the press conference and being able to tell everyone that I was finished playing. Until you have that press conference, it isn't official.

I never thought I would announce my retirement following a Super Bowl win. I just thought it would be after a loss in the playoffs. I had thought it would happen the year before. I was thinking so many negative thoughts about when and how it was going to happen. To do it after winning the Super Bowl was the ultimate. It was definitely a dream come true.

When I got into the locker room it was crazy. There was so much going on. All of the guys were hugging each other and celebrating. It was something else. I wanted my family to share in it, but I couldn't even find them at first. I finally found them after we were all off the field and in the locker room. They brought Jada into the locker room to see me. It was such a joy to hold her. Even though she didn't realize what was going on, I wanted her to share it with me. That was pretty cool. She took it like a trouper. I didn't hear a peep out of her.

As soon as I found the rest of my family, the NFL Network wanted me to go to a live interview with my whole family. Things just started to get crazier and crazier. I was heading back to the locker room and they asked me to go do the *Jimmy Kimmel Show*, which was being taped right across the street. I went over there with Antwaan Randle El, and I was still in my uniform.

When I got back everybody had cleared out of the locker room already. All of my teammates were gone, and I was kind of the last one there. It was a weird feeling.

When I left Ford Field, Magic Johnson was hosting a party as a thank-you for me. He wanted to thank me for what I had done and just everything involved with the Super Bowl. I was the only guy on our team who went to it. The rest of the guys went back to the team hotel for the Steelers party. It was weird because normally in a situation like that you are with your teammates right after the game because you have to get on a plane and go. None of the guys were around. It was nice though. I really appreciated Magic doing that for me.

I got back to our hotel and finally got to enjoy things with all my teammates and friends. It was more insanity when we got there, but it was all friends and family of the players and staff, so that made it better. We were around people we knew. People wanted to come over and take a picture with me or get an autograph, and that was neat because those were friends and family of the people I worked with, and that made it special. I got to finally really see Dan Rooney when we got back. I got the chance to thank him for everything. I got the chance to congratulate him for bringing a fifth championship to Pittsburgh and to tell him how special it was for me. It was important for me to see him and talk to him.

There were some celebrities at our party. Kid Rock, Snoop Dogg, Hank Williams Jr., and Michael Keaton were all there. Even if it was just for a brief moment, it was fun to be bigger than the biggest rock stars, musicians, and actors around. Even if it was just for that day, they wanted to meet us, and that was pretty cool.

As crazy as it is, I did get some sleep that night. I slept like a baby.

SUPER BOWL XL VS. SEATTLE AT FORD FIELD, FEBRUARY 5, 2006

	1	2	3	4	Score
Seattle	3	0	7	0	10
Pittsburgh	0	7	7	7	21

Thirteen years worth of hard work and dreams...I still can't believe it!

REFLECTIONS IN THE REARVIEW MIRROR

Here are a couple more nostalgic photos, one of the house in Detroit—that's now abandoned— that I grew up in, and some mementos from my career that my parents keep in their home today. *Photos courtesy of AP/Wide World Photos.*

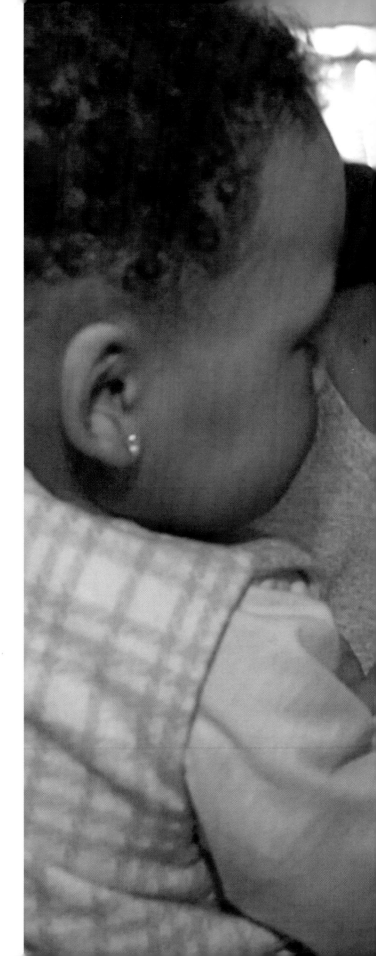

The Insanity Begins

I knew things would get crazy after winning the Super Bowl, but I didn't know it would be as crazy as it turned out to be. I got up the morning after the game and went on *Good Morning America* with Coach Cowher and some of the other guys. That was done really, really early in the morning.

After that we went straight to Orlando, Florida, for the Disney World parade. It was pretty unique. I went there with the thought that it was a parade and there would be people there from all over the country because it's such a destination spot. But I got there and all I saw was a sea of Steelers fans. There were jerseys, hats, and Terrible Towels everywhere. There were so many fans there it was amazing. It was unreal.

We came back to Pittsburgh on Monday night, and Tuesday was our victory parade, with more than 250,000 fans there. I rode in the last car with Trameka. I was in a convertible and got to hold the Lombardi Trophy during the entire parade route. That was amazing to hoist it in the air and show it to the fans for the first time. From the beginning to the end of the parade I didn't think the car was going to be able to get through the parade route because it was so packed. There were people everywhere. The side streets were full, and the crowd was about 10 people deep along the route. Near the end we finally had to get out and walk to the stage because it was so crowded.

When we were up on the stage Coach Cowher addressed the crowd and got them going with the "We dey" chant. It surprised me so much because he is conservative and rarely does anything to upset other teams.

I had a chance to address the crowd, and it was amazing. They were yelling and screaming, and there were people everywhere. My entire career the fans have been my backbone. A lot of the things I do on the field are for the fans in terms of getting them into the game and getting them going. I wanted to tell them thank you. It's not often you get the chance to address the fans, and I really wanted to do it. It was great to see the way the fans came out there to support us.

The next stop for me was Los Angeles to be on the *Tonight Show* with Jay Leno. I was also scheduled to be on the Grammy's with Ben Roethlisberger introducing Kelly Clarkson, but I didn't make it there. Leno was taped right before the Grammy's started, and I had only 30 minutes to get from Glendale, California, to the Staples Center in rush hour traffic at 5:30 with a police escort. It just didn't work. They even held the Grammy's back eight minutes to try and get me there, which is pretty significant in the scheme of things because they don't usually hold those kinds of shows back.

It was wild seeing Ben come out in my Notre Dame jersey on the stage. I had some people come up to me and want to meet me when I finally did get there. I met Kelly, and I talked to Queen Latifah. She congratulated me. I had met her before. I also talked to Nelly and Chris Tucker, who came over and congratulated me. I talked to a bunch of other people, too. It was pretty wild.

From L.A. I went to Tampa to be on the Home Shopping Network. I was on there for an hour selling some autographed memorabilia. I also had the chance to go on *Live with Regis and Kelly*. It was fun because Regis has been a fan of mine since I was at Notre Dame. He is a big Notre Dame guy. I met him at a pep rally at Notre Dame when I was still in school there. It was cool to go on a show like that because it has such a strong following. After that I went on *Fox and Friends* and did an interview there, and finally on the *Tony Danza Show*, which I had done before.

WHAT THE FUTURE HOLDS

During the season I had interviewed with NBC Sports to be part of their coverage for NFL games in the 2006 season. They have the Sunday night game, and I was auditioning for a job on their studio show, *Football Night in America*.

I had also interviewed with some of the other networks and had some different options available.

When the people at NBC heard me on the *Tonight Show* joking about not having a job, they decided they wanted me. I got a call the day after the show with them offering the job. Now, I wanted to see how firm the commitments were with the other networks, but things happened fast with NBC. I started to get a good feeling that it was going to work out with them, and it did.

I ended up flying to Torino, Italy, for the announcement because NBC Sports was there in full force for their broadcast of the Olympics. I did an interview with Bob Costas, who is going to be hosting the Sunday night show and who was there as a studio host for the Olympics. It was wild to make the announcement in that manner. My parents went with me, so it was pretty unique.

The parade back in Pittsburgh was incredible. Trameka and I rode in the final car, and I got to hog the trophy the whole way.

"Here we go, Steelers, here we go!"

REFLECTIONS IN THE
REARVIEW MIRROR

Some family shots in the weeks before Super
Bowl XL. Inside the house, that's my brother
John, dad and mom, sister Kim, aunt Gloria, and
sister-in-law Tracy on the couches, and nephew
Lester, niece Breana, and baby niece Brooke in
my arms. In the picture below, I'm holding Jada
with my family—John, Kimberly, Mom, Dad, and
Trameka at Heinz Field on New Year's Day 2006.

Photos courtesy of the Bettis Family.

Even conservative Coach Cowher got into the spirit of things when he addressed the crowd at the parade, getting everybody fired up with the Bengals' "We dey" chant.

ROLL **B8** SCENE **112** TAKE **7**

FPS CAM

07.20

Dcode™ TS-2 DF DL9400

PROD **ADVAIR**

DIR **G LANKFORD** **45°**

CAM **K McKNIGHT** **1/25/06**

DATE

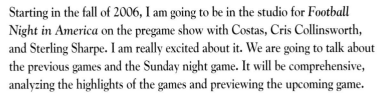

I'm really excited about joining the NBC Sports team. It'll be strange not suiting up for game day every Sunday, but I'm used to being in front of the camera and I think I'm well prepared for the job.

Starting in the fall of 2006, I am going to be in the studio for *Football Night in America* on the pregame show with Costas, Cris Collinsworth, and Sterling Sharpe. I am really excited about it. We are going to talk about the previous games and the Sunday night game. It will be comprehensive, analyzing the highlights of the games and previewing the upcoming game.

I have a lot of television experience, having done my weekly show in Pittsburgh, plus I did a radio show, which helped me as well. I am very prepared for the new job. It's something I have done quite well for a long time, so my confidence level is high. I think I am in good shape in terms of this opportunity because I have been groomed for it for quite a while.

It won't be difficult at all for me to tell it like it is, even when talking about the Steelers. The nature of the business is to call it as you see it, and I have never been afraid to do that. If you look at my track record in Pittsburgh, you'll see that I have always told the truth. Honesty is the best policy, you'll see that and that's what they'll get from me in the booth. If a guy is not playing well, he knows it, and I am just telling the truth and telling what I see. If somebody is struggling, he is struggling, and I will talk about that. My job now is to explore and analyze and not just look at things on the surface and go with the easy answer. I will have to do my homework and research, and I'm prepared to do just that.

It's going to be hard to get used to being in a studio instead of being on the field on game day. It's something that I think I have to do, though. I have run my course. This is the natural progression. It's going to affect me the first couple of Sundays, but I hope I will still be able to be a big part of things. It will help fill the void where I can still be around football and not have to be playing.

In addition to making the announcement, the experience of going to the Olympics was pretty awesome. In the United States we don't realize how big the Olympics are in other parts of the world. We are so programmed with things like the Super Bowl and the World Series that the Olympics are overshadowed. In every other country the Olympics are the equivalent to the Super Bowl and World Series put together. It was a lot bigger than I thought it was. I knew it was big for NBC to fly me there to make the announcement.

While I was in Torino I was on the *Today Show* talking about my new job. When I got to the studio I couldn't believe people watching the taping of the show were holding Terrible Towels. It was amazing that the towel made it all the way to Italy. There really are Steelers fans all over the world.

Thank you, Steelers fans. It's been one heck of a ride.

Thanks for an incredible ride, Steelers fans. So long…